LEARN THE LANGUAGE OF SUCCESS THROUGH POSITIVE DECLARATIONS

TERRI SAVELLE FOY

Contents

Introduction

What exactly is a pep talk? By definition, a *pep talk* is a noun meaning a talk intended to make someone feel more courageous or enthusiastic; a speech of exhortation meant to instill enthusiasm or bolster morale.[1]

Being a former cheerleader, I know a thing or two about pep talks. Cheerleaders are devoted to giving shouts of encouragement to the team they're representing. Coaches give their team locker room pep talks to increase their stamina or restore their determination to get back in the game. Employers give company pep talks to keep morale high and teamwork strengthened.

However, on a day in, day out basis, you're not going to have your own Vince Lombardi or John Maxwell come along and cheer you on to achieve your dreams. I can't show up when your alarm sounds each morning and say, "The secret of your future is in your daily routine! Let's do this!" But everyone needs a pull-yourself-up-by-the-bootstraps pep talk. What does God's Word say we should do?

"David *encouraged himself* in the Lord his God."
– 1 Samuel 30:6 (KJV, emphasis added)

This book is all about *you* giving *yourself* a pep talk consistently and intentionally to achieve *your* dreams! Why? Because your voice is the most influential voice in your life! If you want to see where your life is headed, listen to the words that are coming out of your mouth. Your words are powerful. Your words spoken over yourself are even more powerful! Since I began making positive, faith-filled declarations over myself and my future, I have seen:

- My confidence improve
- My insecurities subside
- My courage go to new heights
- My body get in shape
- My ministry launched
- My marriage restored
- My books in bookstores
- My ministry in France begin and expand
- My ICING Women's Event become a reality
- My finances increase

- My television show air
- My impossible dreams come true before my eyes!

And the same can happen for you!

Through my discipline of speaking daily declarations and faith-filled scriptures, I have more energy now than I did in my twenties, I'm more productive than I was in my thirties, I'm more confident to speak to thousands of people as opposed to shying away from addressing small groups years ago! My marriage has supernaturally been restored when it was on the verge of divorce. I'm happier, I'm healthier, and I attract ideas that produce great wealth. Is it coincidental? Not one bit.

Everything I just shared is a direct result of what I *purposefully* declare out of my mouth consistently. To be honest, I am naturally a shy person who has overcome tremendous insecurities, inferiorities and a compulsive fear of rejection. That may be hard to fathom because I don't exemplify that type of description any more. But it wasn't by accident. *It was completely intentional.*

I have known the power of words my entire life. I grew

up in a strong household of faith and had Proverbs 18:21 memorized by age 5: "Death and life are in the power of the tongue." If you jokingly said, "That scared me to death," or "I nearly died laughing," at our house, you may as well have cussed like a sailor. You would be reprimanded for speaking such damaging words.

If you're just discovering this power you have directly under your nose, then this may sound a little drastic. Let me explain. Matthew 12:34 says, "…for out of the overflow of the heart the mouth speaks" (*Berean Study Bible*). *The Message* translation of verse 37 says, "Words are powerful; take them seriously. Words can be your salvation. Words can also be your damnation." You are truly speaking death or life over your circumstances every time you open your mouth. Many don't realize how detrimental their words are in producing their outcome.

I have heard numerous stories of famous people as well as personal acquaintances who have literally prophesied defeat and in some cases, their own death. If this doesn't send chills up your spine, maybe it will encourage you to zip your lips. The former bass guitarist for the band Weezer, Mikey Welsh, predicted his own death on Twitter based on a dream he had. On September 26, 2011, the 40-year-old musician tweeted, "Dreamt I died in Chicago next weekend (heart attack in my sleep). Need to write my will today." Immediately, he tweeted a correction, "the weekend after next." Two weeks later, on October 8, 2011, Welsh was found dead in a hotel room in Chicago at the exact time he predicted. While prescription drugs were found in his room, the suspected cause of death was a heart attack brought on by drug overdose. What did Matthew 12 say? "Words are powerful; take them seriously."

Another chilling story is taken from Jimi Hendrix lyrics to a song he wrote in September 1965 titled, "The Ballad of Jimi." The lyrics included:

> Many things he would try
> For he knew soon he'd die
> Now Jimi's gone, he's not alone
> His memory still lives on
> Five years, this he said
> He's not gone, he's just dead

Exactly five years later, Hendrix died on September 18,

1970 just as he declared.

One last gripping story to show the seriousness of our words includes a radio interview with former Major League pitcher Frank Pastore. After his baseball career ended, he showcased his talents as a sports celebrity on a daily radio talk show. The last show he taped featured a discussion on the topic of mortality. Pastore said, "You guys know I ride a motorcycle, right? At any moment, especially with the idiot people who cross the diamond lane into my lane...at any minute, I could be spread all over the 210." Eerily, after finishing the show that day, he hopped on his motorcycle and proceeded down his normal route on the 210. Unfortunately, this time, another vehicle swerved head on into his motorcycle...which led to his death.[2]

These are pretty dramatic stories of people prophesying their deaths. You may or may not be using words that detrimental, but what are you saying? Are you speaking words of failure over your future? Are you agreeing with hopelessness? Are you declaring that poverty and defeat are your lot in life? Are you speaking words that are contrary to God's best for your life? I don't want to startle you with this book, but I do want to wake you up to the reality that your words are dictating the life you live today.

"Don't use your words to describe your situation; use your words to change your situation!"
– Joel Osteen

There are always two voices competing for your attention: the voice of faith and the voice of doubt. You cannot talk defeat and expect victory. Your words have creative power. If your dreams and goals appear absolutely hopeless and there is no indication that things will ever improve, as Joel Osteen says, "Don't use your words to *describe* your situation, use your words to *change* your situation!"

I'm so grateful that my parents taught me the power of the tongue, and I've done my best to guard my mouth from speaking death or detrimental words over myself. However, I didn't necessarily practice the habit of doing the opposite: *proactively speaking positive words over my future* or giving myself a pep talk! At least, not with any intentional effort.

Like the Lord told Joyce Meyer, "Joyce, you have stopped saying *negative* things, but you have not started saying *positive* things." It's one thing to stop speaking negative, debilitating words over yourself, but you've got to take it a step further by *replacing* those words with positive declarations over yourself and your future.

What are you saying about your life? Your finances? Your family? Your health? Your career? Your very own words shape your world.

- "I'll never live in a house like that!"
- "I'll never have that kind of salary!"
- "I'm always sick."
- "I have a slow metabolism."
- "I'll never get promoted at this rate!"
- "I've reached my limits."
- "I'm not qualified."
- "I'm too afraid to step out and do something different."
- "I'll always be in debt!"
- "No matter what I try, I can't lose weight!"
- "I could never be friends with them."

- "I'm too shy."

You have the ability to change the entire direction of your life with that little thing under your nose. It's as simple as it seems. Successful people take a proactive approach to their dreams. They don't wait to see what happens with their lives. They prophesy their future. Unsuccessful people speak of things the way they are *as if* they will always be that way. And the truth is, as long as you continue to declare negative statements over your life, then that's exactly what you will continue to experience.

What would happen if you traded all those limiting, debilitating thoughts about yourself, your body, your finances, your career, your marriage, your children, and your future with positive, motivational declarations of hope and faith? Your life would move in that direction.

If your first image of giving yourself a pep talk reminds you of *Saturday Night Live*'s Stuart Smalley and his catchphrase, "I'm good enough. I'm smart enough, and doggone it, people like me," then you probably think this is some kind of ridiculous skit or joke you're playing on yourself. I understand. However, you can't argue with results. When you've experienced dream after dream occur in your life as a result of speaking them out loud, you actually don't think ol' Stuart is so crazy. But be encouraged, I do not sit in front of a mirror and slowly talk to myself (with a lisp)!

In 2007, I made a list of declarations to begin speaking over myself. To begin with, most (if not all) of these positive statements were the *opposite* of what I was experiencing at the time. They were written and spoken by faith! Some of them included:

- "I am proactive."
- "I am in the best shape of my life."
- "I am bold and courageous."
- "I am a voice impacting France for Jesus."
- "I am confident to minister on television."
- "I am confident to minister to thousands of people."
- "I speak at the largest conferences in the world."

When I began this demonstration of faith, I had never ministered in the nation of France, and the largest crowd I had ever spoken to was probably about 300 people.

However, each morning before I would jump in my car and go to the office, I would go in my guest bedroom, grab my *homemade* notebook of declarations and speak them out by faith.

We see this written in Isaiah 46:10 that God "declares the end from the beginning." That's exactly what you're doing when you declare your dreams before they happen.

I'll never forget the evening of March 12, 2012, as I stood on the front row of the largest evangelical church in the nation of France. As I was preparing to take the stage, my daughter, Kassidi, leaned over to me and asked, "Mama, are you a little nervous?" Rightfully so, as I was preparing to minister to approximately 10,000 people in Paris, France. I answered, "I am confident to minister to thousands of people. I speak at the largest conferences in the world."

Why would I reply so courageously? Because what you repeatedly hear, you eventually believe! And you believe your own voice more than anyone's. When you consistently give yourself a pep talk by declaring what you believe about yourself instead of what you feel, eventually, your actions will line up with your words!

In addition to positive declarations, there is nothing more powerful than speaking God's Word out of your mouth. If you're wondering what God's will is for your life, His Word is His will. When you align your mouth with what God's Word says, you are activating the power of God to go to work in your life.

This book is focused specifically on goal-driven declarations in the areas of freedom, faith, finances, family, fitness and your future (dreams and goals). In each section, you will be inspired by others' stories of victory from practicing personal pep talks (through positive declarations and speaking God's Word). I have provided samples of declarations and scriptures for each section in order to get you started down the road of success.

So, what do you want to see happen in your life? Whatever it is, start speaking it out. Declare the end from the beginning. If you'll change what you're saying, you'll change what you're seeing!

Chapter One
Do You Even Know What You're Saying?

**"Whoever guards his mouth and tongue
keeps his soul (life) from troubles."**
– Proverbs 21:23

Words. When was the last time you read an entire book focused on your words? Probably never. In fact, research shows that 2000 words account for 95% of the vocabulary used in daily conversations[3] proving that you don't need to know tens of thousands of words to be an English communicator. It's not how many words you use; it's HOW you use them!

Apparently, women use more words than men—13,000 words *more per day* to be exact. Shocking, I know. Girls learn to speak earlier and more quickly than boys speaking about 20,000 words per day with guys speaking approximately 7,000! Scientists believe it's because higher levels of the protein Foxp2, known as the "language protein,"[4] are found in the female brain. You just thought girls had the gift of gab, but now we can silence men with science!

Think about the most popular word on the planet, OK? That's it. OK. Apparently, it is the most frequently spoken (or typed) word across the globe in languages all over the world, according to Allan Metcalf, author of *OK: The Improbable Story of America's Greatest Word*. OK is used to imply *all right or acceptable*, no matter what language you speak. However, what is not OK is that language experts do not agree about where the word came from. Some say it was derived from a railroad worker named Obadiah Kelly who would put the first letters of his names—O and K— on each object people gave him to send on the train.[5] It was a stamp of approval!

Others say a political organization invented the word when Martin Van Buren was running for President in 1840. They called their group, the O.K. Club, taken from the town where he was born, Old Kinderhook, New York.

Experts do not agree with its origin, but they do agree that the word is purely American and has spread to almost every country on Earth.

You probably use tons of expressions and slang phrases every day that you never even think about. Some of them don't even make sense. They just catch on. Growing up in Fort Worth, Texas, we have our own Southern *slang-uage* (I think I just made up a word). If you're from this neck of the woods, I reckon you're fixin'tuh read some familiar phrases. We use y'all to replace you all or you guys. We use *fixin'tuh* in place of about to. We say *right quick* instead of quickly. Okay, this ain't my first rodeo, I do my best not to sound too Texan when I speak publicly. My point is we tend to grow up speaking certain words and phrases simply because of the environment we live in.

What about common clichés?

Let's not beat around the bush, we've been saying these phrases without a hill a' beans as to what in the world they mean. But we'll say them until the cows come home! How many clichés can I put in one paragraph?!

For example, *to bite the bullet*, meaning to knuckle

down and do something you really don't want to do, was a phrase derived in surgical procedures before the use of anesthetic. Surgeons would operate on wounded soldiers giving them a bullet to bite on in order to distract from the pain.

Cat got your tongue? This is used when someone is silent on a matter. But do you know where its disgusting origin came from? It stems from Middle Eastern punishment when liars' tongues were ripped out of their mouths and fed to the King's cats!

Spilling the beans means to tell a secret. This originated from Ancient Greek voting practices when black and white beans were used to represent yes or no decisions on the issues addressed. Voters would put one colored bean into the pot, and the results were revealed by spilling the beans.

Butter someone up means to impress someone with flattery. This stems from a customary religious act in Ancient India when the devout would literally throw butter balls at the statues of their gods to seek forgiveness and favor!

Don't throw the baby out with the bathwater means don't

get rid of the valuable things along with the unnecessary ones. This origin is as surprising as it is repulsive. In the early 1500's, people only bathed once a year! If that's not filthy enough, families also bathed in the same water without changing it! The adult men would bathe first, then the women, finishing off with the children and then the babies to go last. By the time the babies were bathed, the water was clouded with dirt, scum and filth. The mothers had to take extra care that their babies were not thrown out with the bathwater!

Give them the cold shoulder meaning to be slightly rude or anti-social toward someone. This medieval England custom was used to give a guest a cold piece of meat from the shoulder of the pork or beef when the host felt it was time for the guest to leave. It was a subtle way of saying, "It's time to go."

If you grew up in the *Sesame Street* generation, you might remember one of the Muppet characters using the magical phrase, *Abracadabra!* Poof! Things would appear. I recently heard that this word has its origin in the Aramaic language meaning "what I speak is what I create." How true it is!

My point in sharing these familiar catchphrases, idioms and even childish terms is that we say things all the time without realizing what their meaning, their origin and even their impact is on our lives.

> **"A fool's mouth is his destruction,
> and his lips are the snare of his soul."**
> – Proverbs 18:7

Just as ridiculous clichés are that we say for years having no idea what they literally mean, the same is true with negative statements. How many times have you caught yourself saying things such as:

- "You're killing me!"
- "I would die for that!"
- "I died laughing."
- "That makes me sick!"
- "I'd have a heart attack if I ever did that!"
- "That totally blows my mind!"

Okay, I'm not trying to get too nit-picky over everything

you say, but I do want you to pay attention to words and phrases that don't benefit you. In fact, if your words aren't taking you closer to your dreams, then they could be taking you away from them. Think of these negative, demoralizing statements often heard:

- "I could never afford something like that."
- "That's too expensive for me."
- "I never get any good breaks."
- "I'm just unlucky."
- "I can't lose weight no matter what I try."
- "I could never make that much money."
- "I'd never get that job!"
- "I could never live in a house like that!"

Stop all those "I could never" statements from coming out of your mouth. You are limiting yourself by your vocabulary. Your words are keeping you locked in the very circumstances you want out of! And many times, it's simply a result of our environment. We get accustomed to our friends and relatives talking a certain way. Without thinking anything of it, we chime right in, "Yep, the economy is getting worse and worse. I'll probably get laid off."

I'm sure you've heard of the Miranda Rights which include the statement, "Anything you say can and will be held against you." It's true. If you don't want your words to materialize, then don't speak them. They really will be held against you!

Like White on Rice

Let me illustrate a very famous experiment on the power of words performed by Dr. Mararu Emoto using water over cooked rice. Dr. Emoto used three different containers with three different labels for each. He filled each container with cooked rice and then labeled them: "Thank You," "You're An Idiot," and left one unlabeled.

Every day for one solid month, Dr. Emoto would speak to the container based on the labels. He spoke pleasant, affirming words to the rice labeled, "Thank You." He yelled harsh, demeaning words to the "You're An Idiot" jar; and the third jar, he simply ignored altogether. After thirty days of consistent treatment, the "Thank You" rice began to ferment, look appealing and give off a strong, pleasant aroma. The "You're An Idiot" rice turned mostly black and mushy giving off a sour milk aroma, and the neglected rice simply began to rot and mold turning a disgusting greenish-blue color.

Since then, other scientists, college students and even homeschoolers have duplicated this experiment witnessing the same or similar results proving how powerful your words are in producing the outcome in your life. Words are carriers of life or death. If rice can be affected by positive and negative words as well as total neglect, then how much more can your circumstances be dramatically affected by the same?

Words are vehicles taking you closer to or further from your dreams! My question for you is this: Are your words limiting you or are they promoting you? Are your words demoralizing and destructive or are they courageous and constructive?

Is This a Bunch of Baloney?

Baloney or *bologna* is a kind of sausage made from innards or lowly scraps of meat cuts. It's developed into a slang phrase, *a bunch of baloney*, to imply nonsense.

When you first start studying the importance of your words (making affirmations work and changing your internal dialogue), you will probably encounter skeptics who will unashamedly warn you that "it's a bunch of baloney" or nonsense.

The internet is filled with claims of people insisting that they have never gotten the results they hoped for by making positive affirmations! You may even encounter friends who assure you, "I tried that. It doesn't work." Some may say, "That works for some people but not me. I'm just unlucky." Some will proclaim, "It's a waste of time. It won't work."

There's one thing these people don't understand. It is working! They are using affirmations and getting exactly what they are affirming and declaring. They're just using them negatively. Why not use your words to help you rather than hinder you? Your words can literally guide you to your heart's desires, dreams and goals.

You Are Here!

If you spend much time at the local shopping mall but are directionally challenged (okay, I'm describing myself), you'll notice several directory signs placed throughout the mall mapping the various locations. In order to pinpoint your present location, there's typically a star or a big circle with the words, "You are here." Once you locate your current spot on the map, the next step is to identify the destination you want to reach. Then you simply follow the steps outlined on the map.

This book is a directory, so-to-speak. I want you to identify where you are in life. Is your body out of shape? Are your finances a big mess? Is your marriage failing? Is your career nonexistent or miserable? Is your dream somewhere off in space, not even close to being a reality? Then you need to seriously locate where you are today.

Next, pinpoint your desired destination. Proverbs 29:18 says, "Where there is no vision, the people perish" (KJV). If you don't have a vision, you're dying. Plain and simple. You must identify the vision or destination you want to reach. If your vision is to reach a financial goal, then you need to be very specific about it. We are instructed in Habakkuk 2:2 to write the vision plainly on paper. I'm a stickler for having dreams and goals in writing. Vague goals produce vague results. It's not enough to only say,

"I am believing for financial increase." That's no different than looking at the mall directory and saying, "I want to go to women's fashion." No, you're crystal clear on which women's fashion store you want to browse. Equally, you need to be laser-focused and crystal clear on your financial destination. For example, "I am saving $10,000 this year."

In order to start putting one foot in front of the other and taking steps to reach this destination, you begin by speaking it out! Romans 4:17 says to speak of "nonexistent things AS IF they already exist" (AMPC, emphasis added). You're practicing God's Word each time you speak it out. Yes, you may feel like a nut the first time or two you do this, but you already sound like a nut saying, "Cat got your tongue?" And you don't even really know what you're saying! The difference is now your words are acting as a tool, a vehicle, to get you closer to your dreams! Why wouldn't you choose to feel like a nut in the privacy of your own home? Trust me, this nut gets results, and you will too.

Proactively go after your dreams with the words of your mouth. Let your words move you towards what you want, not what you don't want.

Change Your Words, Change Your World

There is a story (that's gone viral on YouTube) about a blind man sitting on the pavement in front of a government building. He has a homemade sign that reads, "I'm blind. Please help." Most people hastily pass by the man without much notice. He receives a few measly donations. Then a young professional lady stops in front of him and reads his sign. With worn hands, the blind man feels her shoes to get an idea of who is standing in front of him. She bends down, picks up his sign, flips it over and begins to write. Afterwards, she places the sign back in its place and leaves. Then something remarkable happens. People stop to read the sign, and they begin making considerable donations.

At the end of the day, the young professional returns. When she approaches the man, he reaches out and recognizes the feel of her shoes then asks, "Miss, please tell me. What did you write on my sign?"

She says, "I wrote the same thing; I just used different words." The camera then zooms in on the blind man's sign that reads, "It's a beautiful day, but I can't see it." The video ends with this powerful declaration: change your words, change your world.[6]

Just as a simple change of words changed the blind man's outcome, the same will happen for you.

**"A fool's mouth is his destruction,
and his lips are the snare of his soul."**
– Proverbs 18:7

Chapter Two
Program Your Mind for Greatness

**"The heart of the wise teaches his mouth,
and adds learning to his lips."**
– Proverbs 16:23

What if I told you that what you say to others isn't nearly as important as what you say to yourself? It's true. How you talk to yourself will determine how successful you will be. Period. That's a bold statement full of truth. Your personal pep talk can help you lose weight, get good grades, achieve promotion, close sales, get along with family members, win awards and even gold medals!

In 1993[7], national champion figure skaters were interviewed for a study on their unique coping strategies for handling stress. They discovered 158 unique strategies, but the most common used by 76% of the skaters was "rational thinking and self-talk."

Ruben Gonzalez agreed with this study and took his personal list of positive affirmations with him all over the world. Regularly, he gave himself a pep talk helping him become "resilient in the face of life's challenges." Reading what he called "The Champion's Creed"[8] helped him stay focused on his goals and become a three-time Olympic medalist. Gonzalez believes that in order to start your day like a champion, you must fine-tune your mindset. He recommends reading positive, motivational statements like "The Champion's Creed" aloud first thing in the morning and before bed with power, passion, and eyeball-to-eyeball in the mirror.

The Champion's Creed
by Ruben Gonzalez

I am a champion.
I believe in myself. I have the will to win.
I set high goals for myself.
I surround myself with winners.
I'm cool, positive, and confident.

I'm willing to pay the price of success.
I stay relaxed and in control at all times.
I focus all my energy on the job at hand.
I take responsibility for all of my results.
I have the courage to endure and persist.
I vividly imagine what victory will feel like.
I am a champion and I ***will*** win.

Do you talk to yourself? Of course you do. Perhaps you haven't voiced the internal dialogue in your head like I'm suggesting, but you do talk to yourself whether you've realized it or not. We all have an inner voice—the voice in your mind that speaks without you even recognizing it. It's a running commentary you have with yourself, most frequently about yourself.

In fact, we are all in a constant state of internal dialogue. I read where brain research has discovered that we send ourselves messages at a rate of nearly 500 words per minute.[9] That's a lot of chatter going on inside that nobody hears...except you. But it's not mindless chatter. It has a way of creating its own reality. If you dwell on negative thoughts, they will stop you from reaching your dreams. In fact, your mind can literally talk you out of your destiny!

What we tell ourselves determines our failures and our successes. Unfortunately, most of our internal conversation is negative. Many of us are still riddled with guilt over our past mistakes or we struggle with anxiety or fear about the future.

Your self-talk determines how you see yourself, how you feel about yourself and even how others view you. What you say to yourself determines your outcome in life. If your running internal dialog is mostly negative, then you will have a negative life. If your inner conversation is hopeful, optimistic and uplifting, you will live a positive life. I want you to use your self-talk to your advantage.

> **"I'm always in conversation,**
> **and sometimes other people are involved."**
> – Mark Twain

You and you alone hold the power to change. God will not do for you what you can do for yourself. In fact, Joshua 3:4 says, "You have not passed this way before."

In other words, new seasons are coming your way, new opportunities are on the horizon, new beginnings are in your future, but you have to do your part. You have to get your thinking, your internal dialogue and your self-talk in line with God's thoughts about you.

The first step to improvement is becoming conscious of what you're saying in your mind about yourself and to yourself. What have you told yourself today? Are you affirming things such as:

- "I look fat."
- "I'll never get married."
- "I'm terrible at making friends."
- "I'm insecure."
- "I could never get promoted."
- "I'll never get out of debt."
- "I'm not capable of being successful."
- "I look old."
- "I'm scared to try something new."
- "I'm afraid I'll fail."

The silent conversation you carry on with yourself

affects everything in your life. It impacts your self-esteem, your confidence (or lack of it), your relationships, your career choice, your health, your well-being, your mood, your attitude, your children, your relationship with God and your ability to fulfill your purpose in life.

I heard an interesting story about a university professor who made a unique offer to his college students one day. As he was getting ready to administer the final exams of the semester, he bragged on how proud he was of the class and said because they had done so well he wanted to offer them something.

He said, "Anyone who would like to receive an automatic C grade on this test, raise your hand." He explained they wouldn't be tested whatsoever. Just lift your hand, no pressure, no failing grade, you'll pass with flying colors. One hand went up, then another, and another until about half of the class got up and walked out of the room. They were so relieved. No stress, no worry, no failing grade.

The professor went on to pass out the test to the rest of the students remaining, but he placed them face down on their desks. He asked them not to turn them over until he instructed them to do so. For the next several minutes, he encouraged them on how they were going to go far in life, and that they should always strive to do their best. Then he instructed them to turn the test over and get started. When they turned over the papers, it had only two sentences: "Congratulations! You just made an A!"

The ones who stayed believed they had what it took to get an A! Why settle for a C when you can get an A? Why settle for mediocrity when God has amazing plans for your life? Why settle for less simply because of your belief system? When you allow negative thoughts to remain in your mind, you're settling for a C! God has so much more for you, but you have to change your internal dialogue.

Your mind will try to talk you out of God's best. You'll consistently feel unqualified, too shy, incapable, unworthy, unskilled, afraid, intimidated, less than average. I'm asking you to believe in yourself a little more. Believe that God's Word is true and that it was written for you. Believe that when you take authority of your thought life and begin speaking faith-filled declarations over yourself, your life is moving in that direction.

"Man's mind may be likened to a garden, which may be intelligently cultivated or allowed to run wild."

– James Allen

Your inner self-talk creates the circumstances of your life. If you want to change your circumstances, then you have to do what God instructs us to do: "Put off the former man and be renewed in the spirit of your mind" (See Ephesians 4:23-24). In order to change your mind, you must change your internal *and* external speech.

The change starts with awareness. You need to be aware of the thoughts that are pervading your mind on an ongoing basis. Are they negative? Are they fearful? Are they thoughts of regret over your past? Are you filled with shameful thoughts? Are you entertaining insecure thoughts? Were you raised with a poverty mentality and entertaining thoughts of never getting ahead financially?

Your internal dialogue is a result of years of input. If you were told negative statements as a child, then you have to retrain your mind to see the unlimited potential God has placed in you through a series of positive input. Taking it a step further, you need to hear yourself declare your worth, your value and your potential.

With your very own positive pep talk, you will literally reprogram your mind for greatness. As you become dedicated to the *consistency* of making positive, faith-filled declarations, it replaces all those damaging, limiting beliefs about yourself with hopeful, unlimited, courageous resolve to be what God created you to be!

Repetition: The Secret to a Successful Pep Talk

My Grandmother, aka Grandma Creech, just turned 87 years old this month. She still mows her own lawn, collects rent from her tenants, drives three hours to visit us, attends church faithfully and even takes meals to the "elderly" in her city! Her mind is sharp, she dresses fashionably, she uses a smart phone (uses is a strong word, let's just say she speaks into it), and she's headed to Hawaii next month for a vacation with the family. I know people in their sixties who are lethargic, complaining of all their aches and joint pains, and act older than my youthful grandmother. But Grandma Creech does have a secret to her fountain of youth. Every single day, for close to sixty years, she never gets out of bed without confessing, "God renews my youth as the eagles." No kidding. Every single day. And she loves to share her secret with anyone who asks. It's an open door for her to preach. But hey, you can't argue with results.

What are you declaring every day, without realizing you're creating your results?

- "I'm so tired."
- "I don't have any energy."
- "I never sleep."
- "I'm always exhausted."
- "Oh my gosh, my back hurts."
- "I'm getting old."

Could it be that what you're repeatedly saying, you're repeatedly experiencing?

Advertisers and marketing campaigns spend billions of dollars planting slogans in our minds. They strategically use the power of repetition to get you to purchase what they're selling. When familiar jingles and phrases get stuck in your head then you've heard them repeated enough to become engrained in your subconscious mind.

- "Be all that you can be." – The United States Army
- "The breakfast of champions." – Wheaties cereal
- "Eat Mor Chikin!" – Chick-fil-A
- "Good to the last drop." – Maxwell House coffee
- "Give me a break, give me a break; break me off a piece of that Kit Kat bar!" – Kit Kat

I have a feeling you sang the last one like I did typing it! If you can recall those advertising slogans, you have practiced the law of repetition without consciously doing so. You didn't sit in front of a mirror and make yourself memorize the campaign phrases. You simply heard them, programmed them and retained them.

Just as learning a foreign language is acquired through repetition of hearing those unfamiliar pronunciations and phonetics, so is reprogramming your mind for success through repetition. Constant repetition is the secret key.

You were born with unlimited potential, but you have to program that into your subconscious mind. We become the programs that we receive *the most*. Every single person has programs that affect their lives. From the moment you were born, every single word you heard, everything you saw, every message you received was typed, so-to-speak, into your personal keyboard (your five physical senses), then those messages were recorded into your hard drive (stored in your brain). The reason this is so important to grasp is because that particular part of the brain doesn't know the difference between what is real or unreal, positive or negative, true or false. It simply records the message that it's told.

The Bible says that your words have the power to curse (put you down) or to bless (pick you up).[10] When you choose to bless your own life by speaking positive, faith-filled declarations out of your mouth, your brain accepts whatever you tell it.

To *affirm* means to make firm. When you affirm and declare by faith: "I am healthy. I am successful. I am peaceful. I am joyful. I am proactive. I am confident. I am highly favored of God," your brain simply believes these things are made firm. Consequently, it starts taking action in that direction. Your brain likes to prove itself right. Whatever instructions you give your brain repeatedly, it likes to go to work to make it happen!

Here's the thing: your brain doesn't care if the

information is positive or negative. It simply receives the message that you tell it and proactively looks for opportunities to make it a reality. Isn't that amazing? When you say, "I can't do this. I never have enough money. I look so old. I hate working out," your statements literally become instructions to your subconscious mind whose duty is to work endlessly to make sure these instructions are carried out.

Again, your brain believes whatever you tell it *the most*. Your repeated thoughts and words shape your life. That's why you must spend time daily declaring your new positive affirmations about yourself and your future. It is only through repetition that you begin to reprogram your mind. You must be willing to be committed, disciplined and determined to change old patterns.

Not only are "old habits hard to break" but so are old patterns of thinking. You can't expect to see a complete turnaround after one day of making positive declarations. It needs to become a part of your daily routine.

How long do I have to do this, Terri? Until you see change. In 2007, I made my personal list of faith-filled declarations, and I committed to speaking them out every single morning during my prayer time. I had already made prayer time a daily priority by then (with no exception) so adding this list wasn't difficult, but it was time-consuming, I admit. There are some days I don't want to read the entire lengthy list, so I'll read every other one. But I know it's the consistency of hearing myself speak them out that brought about the change in me and in my circumstances. Repetition is key.

Angels Are Activated by Your Words

The Bible reveals to us that angels are literally at your disposal waiting for your command. You may or may not find this hard to believe, but I can prove it from God's Word. Psalm 103:20 says, "Bless the Lord, ye His angels, that excel in strength, that do His commandments, HEARKENING UNTO THE VOICE OF HIS WORD" (KJV, emphasis added).

How do you activate angels on your behalf? This verse revealed that angels *hearken* (listen, giving respectful attention) unto the voice of the Lord—unto His Word. Angels still do this today. God gives instructions to His angels, and they carry them out. When we speak God's

Word, we release angels to go to work on our behalf. However, when we speak contrary to the Word of God, we prevent angels from benefiting our lives.

The truth is that when you speak God's Word out of your mouth, you have the ear of Almighty God. He loves nothing more than to hear His children speak His Word back to Him. When you speak the name of Jesus, all of Heaven stands at attention.

I always begin my declarations by saying, "In the name of Jesus, I declare..." because scripture tells us that no man can get to the Father except through Jesus. This book isn't about you practicing mind science, mind over matter or some psychology game you're playing with yourself. It's about calling on Heaven to aid you in becoming everything Jesus died to give you. It's about you seeing yourself the way God sees you, doing what God wants you to do and speaking the way God wants you to speak. And this can be done "in the name of Jesus!"

**"Pleasant words are like a honeycomb,
sweetness to the soul and health to the bones."**
– Proverbs 16:24

Chapter Three
The Language of Success

**"A man will be satisfied with good
by the fruit of his mouth…"**
– Proverbs 12:14

At the time I'm writing this portion of the book, I am sitting in a hotel room in Milan, Italy where my daughter recently signed a contract for modeling in the *fashion capital*. We arrived four days ago on a fourteen-hour journey from Dallas, dropped off our bags at the hotel, took a taxi to the modeling agency and hit the ground running. Unfortunately, they gave us very little instructions on where to go, what to do and how to do it. They assumed we spoke their language: Italian fashion, that is.

One person told us to take the metro from casting to casting, another said to take the tram and another the bus. We didn't know where any of them were or how to obtain a transportation pass so we jumped in taxis from job site to job site. Because we didn't speak the language and we had no instruction, we wasted a lot of time and a lot of euros trying to get to our destinations.

As each day went by and we were immersed in the Italian lifestyle and lingo, we began to learn the system. We figured out how to obtain the *Azienda Transporti Milanesi* (metro card), how to pinpoint our destination for the trains and follow the advice of Google Maps guiding us from the M1 to the M3, walk 800 kilometers, jump on the city tram in the direction of San Babila and you're there. *E' facile.* (It's easy!)

I've discovered that if you want to be successful in achieving your dreams, you will need to learn what could be a foreign language to you: the language of success. Dream achievers speak an entirely different vocabulary. What is this language? They speak of their dreams *before* they manifest AS IF they already have them. They literally give themselves a pep talk about their potential!

If you only knew how many times I have walked into a local bookstore, pointed to the shelves and declared by faith, "My books are sold on these bookshelves in Jesus' name!" What you repeatedly hear, you eventually believe! I was calling things that be not as if they already are! As you can imagine, my books are now sold in those bookstores! In fact, I took a photo of me standing in the very bookstore where I used to just point to the shelf and declare my dream, but now, I'm holding my book with the proof. There's power in your words!

It's time for you to learn this foreign language, this language of success. It is the language of God in which you no longer speak of the problem, you speak of the solution. Literally, you prophesy your future. You proactively go after your dreams with the words of your mouth. It will save you years of frustration over dreams delayed!

In the beginning, you may feel like Kassidi and I did when we arrived in Milan. It's foreign. It's strange. It doesn't make sense to your mind. But once we immersed ourselves in the culture, it became common sense. The same is true when you immerse yourself in God's Word, it will become first nature for you to declare your desires, your dreams and your destiny before they happen!

God always places a bigger dream in your heart before you have the ability to achieve it. Speaking your dreams into existence is part of the process in achieving them. We see this in Hebrews 11:3, "By faith we understand that the worlds were framed by the word of God, so that the things which are seen were not made of things which are visible." This entire world was created with words. God said, "Let there be" and there was (the sun, the moon, the stars, everything).[11] In fact, the Bible tells us that we serve a God who speaks of "nonexistent things" AS IF they already exist.[12] He expects us to apply the same principle.

Start speaking of nonexistent things as if they already exist:

- "I am a best-selling author."
- "I am the owner of a dance studio."
- "I am leading a department."
- "I am a championship boxer."
- "I am the best fitness instructor."
- "I am debt-free."
- "I am pastoring the greatest church."
- "I am the top sales winner in our organization."
- "I am happily married."
- "I am carrying a healthy baby."

Proverbs 13:3 says, "He who guards his mouth preserves his life...." In other words, you may think your dreams will never come to pass, but don't speak it. You may think you're not qualified for the promotion, but don't speak it! You may think you'll never record an album, but don't speak it. You may think that your business won't take off for another ten years, but don't speak it. Why? Your words have power.

> **"Your dreams could be delayed**
> **because of what you're saying."**
> – Joel Osteen

In my book, *Dream it. Pin it. Live it. Make Vision Boards Work for You*, I dedicated an entire chapter on making positive declarations over your dreams and goals. I am absolutely convinced that getting clear on your dreams and writing them down are vital keys to success, but that's not enough. What's coming out of your mouth has everything to do with what you are experiencing.

For example, back in 2012 I made my first vision board. I've had my personal dreams and goals in notebooks for years, but I actually made my first vision board in 2012. I had fun dreaming as big as I could, cutting out pictures and pinning them all over this 20 x 30 cork board in my office.

My board contained specific dreams such as:

- A super-imposed picture of leadership expert and best-selling author, John Maxwell and me posing together with the declaration, "I speak at events with John Maxwell" (whom I had never met).
- A photo taken of Joyce Meyer's women's conference in a coliseum (taken from her website) with the declaration, "I speak to thousands of people" (which I had never done).
- A map of France with the declaration, "My books are translated in French" (when I didn't have or even know any French publishers).
- A photo of the Dallas Cowboys Cheerleaders (No, I'm not still dreaming of being a professional cheerleader for the NFL, although my husband assured me that they do select "old ones" from time to time). Instead

of being a cheerleader, I declared, "I minister to the Dallas Cowboys Cheerleaders" (whom I had only seen from a distance and aspired to be as a kid).

These are just a few of the dreams I pinned on my vision board and declared out of my mouth consistently. Remember, designing a vision board is not for the purpose of creating a beautiful piece of art to simply hang on your wall. It's not intended to blend in with the décor of your home or office. Getting the board completed is an amazing feat that most people will never tackle. It demands that you get serious about your future. You get crystal clear on your goals. That's step one.

But you also have to take action towards them. Step two is doing what God's Word instructs us to do in Romans 4:17[13]: call things that be not as though they already were. Every dream I just shared with you has been fulfilled, and many more. And it can happen for you too. Do you know why? Because your words create your world. Your life moves toward the very words you speak. Job 22:28 says, "You will also decide and decree a thing, and it will be established for you; and the light [of God's favor] shall shine upon your ways" (AMPC).

First of all, nothing happens until you decide. Second, you must decree it. The word decree means to decide with authority or to order something. The word establish means to become a common occurrence. In other words, the more you decree it, the more it will be established in your life, and it will become a common occurrence. You could re-write this verse with these definitions inserted, "You will decide to order something with authority, and it will become a common occurrence for you..." I like the sound of that!

Once you get results, you can't stop decreeing, speaking and giving yourself pep talks! Keep on keeping on until it becomes a common occurrence.

One Thing Separates Winners from Losers

I want to mention one more vital step to this overall process of achieving your dream so you never get the impression that you can make a vision board, speak to it for a few weeks or months, and bam! They appear! A crucial step I must mention is found in James 2:17, "Faith alone without works is dead." One translation of *works* is *corresponding action*. Simply put: you must also take action toward your dreams.

> **"The one thing that separates winners from losers more than anything else is winners take action."**
> – Jack Canfield

For example, when my daughter Kassidi had a dream of modeling abroad, she designed her first vision board, pinning all of her dreams and goals. They included opportunities to model in either London, England; Paris, France; or Milan, Italy by the year 2017. She displayed her favorite fashion models, designer brands, and all things modeling, along with some financial and physical goals included. She hung this exhibit of her future aspirations near her bathroom vanity where she routinely gets ready each day and disciplined herself to speak to those dreams every single morning as she was applying her make up. It became a part of her daily schedule. But that's not all.

She began taking action toward the achievement of those goals. She began eating healthier and maintaining a greater diet. She incorporated completely different fitness routines into her lifestyle as opposed to the workouts she had practiced as a competitive cheerleader in the past. It was not easy, by any means. But she remained focused on her dreams by looking at them each morning. She declared them with assurance upon rising each day. Consequently, her actions followed her faith. She began acting as if she were signing a contract to model abroad. She was preparing for the fulfillment of a dream.

Her hard work paid off. Her declarations manifested. She received the phone call that an agency in Milan, Italy wanted to sign with her, and she began working with them in May 2016.

Imagine teaching your children these principles to get them clear on their dreams, declare them out loud with assurance and step out in faith and take action. How much more could our next generation accomplish?

Some dreams will never manifest in your life until you begin speaking them out loud and taking action toward them. That's what Sheriee did in order to have her article published in Oprah Winfrey's magazine:

I've been reading Terri's book, *Dream It. Pin It.*

Live It. Make Vision Boards Work for You, and diligently putting my vision board together. One of the photographs on my board is a picture of a page out of O, The Oprah Magazine, because it is a dream of mine to someday write an article for its readers. Well, I just received an email from the editors of O because they want to feature me in their March issue on the Question page! This may seem like a fluke, but it's not. I've submitted answers for their monthly questions many times before, but *when I added faith and action* with what Terri has taught me, I am now selected for the magazine! And I'm sure this is just the beginning... Thanks Terri, a million times over, for your obedience to minister the gospel and set an example for women like myself.

– Sheriee M.

Remember, take a proactive approach to your dreams! Speak them out BEFORE they happen! When you consistently hear uplifting, positive declarations spoken from your mouth about your future, you will get in agreement with it and eventually experience it!

So, what is the language of success?

Declare the end from the beginning.

– Isaiah 46:10

Declare new things before they happen.

– Isaiah 42:9

Do you want to see where your life is headed? Listen to the words that are coming out of your mouth.

Chapter Four
Speak What You Believe—
Believe What You Speak

"And since we have the same spirit of faith, according to
what is written, 'I *believed*, and therefore I *spoke*,' we also
believe and therefore *speak*."
– 2 Corinthians 4:13 (emphasis added)

In order to achieve anything in your life, you must *believe*.
If you want to see results from speaking to your dreams,
you absolutely must believe in the power of your words.

Back in 1969, when my dad first heard a minister
named Kenneth Copeland preach the gospel, he was very
skeptical of these "faith teachers." He thought all ministers
were cons only out for people's hard-earned money.
My mom dragged him to a meeting Mr. Copeland was
conducting in Shreveport, Louisiana and said, "Please
just listen to this man. If you don't get anything out of it, I

promise I won't make you go to another church service."

Reluctantly, my dad agreed to go. But as he sat there, actually listening for the first time rather than counting the minutes until the final "amen," Kenneth Copeland got his attention like no other preacher ever had. In fact, his closing remarks sealed the deal. Mr. Copeland grabbed the podium with both hands like he was riding a Harley-Davidson motorcycle, looked at the congregation and said, "If you believe it, it'll work. If you don't, it won't. Goodnight." And he walked off the stage.

I could sum up this entire book with Mr. Copeland's final statement that night. If you believe in the power of speaking God's Word and positive declarations over yourself, you will get positive results. If you speak it, but don't believe in what you're speaking, you won't see the positive results you desire. If you believe it, it'll work. If you don't, it won't. Goodnight.

Knee Patients Healed Through Believing

In a well-known study involving 180 patients[14] with knee pain, doctors randomly separated them into three groups: one group would receive surgery to cut away and remove loose cartilage; the second would undergo arthroscopic lavage (in which bad cartilage would be flushed out); and the third group would have the signs of surgery but no actual treatment.

The patients in the third group who underwent the pretend surgery received anesthesia and incisions on the knee, as if to insert surgical instruments. The remarkable thing is that two years later, without any knowledge of the actual procedure done to them, patients who received absolutely no treatment whatsoever reported the *same amount of relief* as those who received actual treatments. Doctors concluded from their experiment that the brain believed and expected it would be healed, so it was.

You must believe God's Word is true. You must believe that what you're speaking will manifest. You may recall the story of Abraham being told by God that he would be the father of many nations. Considering that Abraham was impotent up to that point in his life and his wife, Sarah, had already undergone the change of life, it was what some would label unbelievable. However, the Bible says, "When there was nothing left to hope for, Abraham still hoped and *believed*. As a result, he became a father of many nations, as he had been told" (Romans 4:18 GW, emphasis added).

He hoped, he believed and he became.

When you get to a place in your life where it appears nothing is going in your favor, your circumstances seem hopeless and you have no indication that things will ever change; however, you say with great assurance, "I BELIEVE" then you better get ready, you are speaking the language of God!

> **"My doctor told me I would never walk again.
> My mother told me I would. I believed my mother."**
> – Wilma Rudolph,
> (U.S. Olympic Games winner of three Gold medals in
> Track and Field and considered the "fasted woman in the
> world" in the 1960's)

Let's look at how God moved in Jessica's family when she aligned her words with the language of God:

At what should have been the joyful sonogram of our third child, a battle began in our family—

both spiritually and physically. Minutes into the ultrasound, the technician pointed something out. Something I was unprepared for. Our baby had two club feet, a condition I'd heard of but didn't understand. The technician explained that the bones in our baby's feet were growing inward, curled at the ankles toward each other.

The devil immediately started playing with my mind. Information was tossed around about specialist sonograms and at what point the baby would be able to walk after treatments, but I couldn't focus on anything except not crying— which is a task in and of itself for a pregnant woman.

As soon as the appointment ended, I rushed to the bathroom to take control of my emotions. I was helpless to fix my baby, but with God, ALL things are possible. I literally got on my knees on the bathroom floor, sobbing and crying out to a God Who is bigger than club feet. He, and

He alone, could fix this. My baby would not be crippled.

From that day forward my husband and I declared daily that our baby would have strong and straight ankles and feet.

At our specialist ultrasound months later, everything appeared the same. And it could have shaken my faith in my son's healing. It almost did. But the following Sunday, basking in praise and worship to the song God Is Able, I heard God speak to me. "Don't give up on me." He said, "I am still strong. I am still bigger than club feet. Continue to believe for this healing."

Letting the tears freely fall, I made the determination to never give up on Him. God has shown Himself so faithful to us in every area of our lives. Why give up now?

Every day, I spoke it. Every day, I believed it. *God is*

able. He will never fail. He is almighty God. Greater than all we seek, Greater than all we ask. He has done great things. God is with us. God is on our side. He will make a way. Far above all we know, Far above all we hope, He has done great things... He will never fail us...For the Lord, our God is able.

The song became the anthem of my pregnancy.

And yes, Lucas was born with two club feet. Again, I could have lost faith. I could have let it break me. But this time, it didn't even come close. God proved Himself faithful every day. He sent us to the perfect pediatric orthopedic specialist who explained the typical procedures for treatment of club feet. The treatments were $12,000. Our boy is worth every penny. But God showed Himself to us again. The very specialist we met with, out of all the six specialists at the hospital, was the one who had connections at Texas Scottish Rite Hospital—a children's hospital that gives treatment at NO CHARGE! They're main requirement is a referral from a pediatrician.

An application and referral process that usually takes over a week—which would have been too late for best results—took no time at all. The specialist we met with called the referral in while we were still in his exam room, and the nurse came in with an appointment time for two days later.

It turned out the children's hospital also offered a second option for treatment that was less intrusive on Lucas. Physical therapy using splints and exercises. My job was by far more intensive but we felt peace about the physical therapy option. We continued to confess daily that he has strong and straight ankles and feet. Every night as we prayed over him, we would declare that he runs and doesn't grow weary, he walks and he doesn't faint.

Two years of therapy that could have been exhausting, turned into precious one-on-one time between me and my third born. God provided every ounce of grace our family needed to make it through the process. And at our last appointment, the orthopedic surgeon told me, "You've made it!"

Lucas is an active four-year-old who runs everywhere he goes! He makes it up and down the stairs. He kicks soccer balls through the house. All things they said could be difficult for him to do.

Our house is filled with the pitter patter of Lucas' little feet—his strong and straight ankles and feet. What a beautiful sound it is.

– Jessica S., Texas

Voice Your Bold Faith

In Acts 27, we see the story of Paul on a ship that encountered hurricane-like storms. The others onboard were terrified and convinced they wouldn't survive. The storm was severe, frightening and death-defying. Right in the midst of this horrific turbulence, Paul gave his own pep talk whether they wanted to hear it or not, "...Be of good cheer, for I believe God" (Verse 25 KJV). That's bold faith right there!

How could Paul say such a thing? He had so much unwavering confidence in God's Word that he refused to believe anything but God's promises to us. What are His promises? Hebrews 13:5 says, "I will not, I will not, I will not in any degree leave you helpless…" (AMPC). When God says something once, He means it. When He says it three times, He is trying to get our attention. If you believe His Word, then find a Scripture that declares His promises over your life and declare it!

This is such a lesson for us. When outward appearances look contrary to the dreams on your vision board, when your circumstances are tragic, trying and draining you of emotional strength, that's when you need to declare with even more fervency, "I believe!"

Notice Paul didn't just think it, he spoke it. His words brought comfort, confidence and courage! Your words will do the same thing when you speak them out into the atmosphere. You can literally change the environment with your words.

For example, our ministry requires a great deal of finances each month to maintain and support our outreaches into the girls' homes and safe houses, television and missions; however, God said in Philippians 4:19 that He will supply ALL of our needs. All means everything. When needs arise, when bills are due, when God gives us a new assignment, I say, "Lord, You said that You would supply ALL, so I believe!" And you know what? He does month after month. I love what Jesse Duplantis says, "Your job is to believe that God can do His job!" Declare, "I believe!"

One of the most powerful things you can do is hear yourself declare the Word of God out loud. Your ears need to hear what your mouth is professing!

Everything Is Possible for One Who Believes

God has made it simple for you to receive your breakthrough. All you have to do is believe that His Word is true, speak what you believe, and believe what you speak. All that's needed is your declaration made in faith. (See Romans 10:6–10.)

"Have faith in God," Jesus answered. "Truly I tell you, if anyone *says* to this mountain, 'Go, throw yourself into the sea,' and *does not doubt* in their heart but *believes* that what they say will happen, it will be done for them. Therefore I tell you, whatever you ask for in prayer, *believe* that you have received it, and it will be yours" (Mark 11:23-24 NIV, emphasis added).

Did you notice that the word PRAY is not in this verse, but the word SAY is? It doesn't say he shall have whatever he PRAYS. It says he shall have whatever he SAYS. Kenneth Hagin said, "Faith will work by SAYING it or by PRAYING it. But when you pray it, you still have to SAY it."

These two verses (Mark 11:23-24) brought Kenneth Hagin out of bed from near-complete paralysis, due to an incurable blood disease and two serious organic heart problems, to traveling the world preaching the gospel, totally made whole. He admitted that he was healed by a combination of the two: He prayed. Then he didn't just think it, but he said out loud, "I BELIEVE that I receive healing for my body."[15]

There are seven simple words from Mark 9:23[16] that are often overlooked and disregarded as impossible. But I want you to get these seven words engrained in your thinking with no exceptions. "Everything is possible for one who *believes*." For who? The one who believes. Everything?

Does that mean everything but weight loss? No, everything! Everything but financial goals? Everything! That includes your marriage restoration, baby conceived, children serving God, business flourishing, physical body made whole, emotional stability, custody awarded, stolen years restored! Everything means everything, but the responsibility is yours to believe!

Cheryl believed God could turn her life around, and look what happened against all odds:

> Dear Terri, I don't know if words can express how grateful and blessed I am by your teaching. You have shown me in easy, simple steps how to truly set goals and see them achieved. I am truly motivated and inspired not only to dream again, but to actually *believe* it could happen.
>
> December of 2014, against all odds, I got custody of my granddaughters and brought them home to live with me. I *believed* God would provide. I am now living in an apartment (with three bedrooms, so that each girl has her own room). All of my

family said there was no way I could afford it. God has blessed and provided so much that I have been able to pay off all my credit cards, have some money in savings and get a newer car (that doesn't always need repairs).

I had been taught for years in business about setting goals and had never been able to do it. I had just let life happen to me. But now, thanks to your inspiration, I am setting goals and choosing what I will do with my life. You make it simple and easy. I almost feel silly that I made it seem so hard... that it was beyond what I could do.

Thank you for having the dream and vision to teach people. It has forever changed my life.

– Cheryl B., Minnesota

Become What You Believe

There's a story in Matthew[17] of two blind men approaching Jesus crying out, "Mercy, Son of David! Mercy on us!" They were asking Jesus to give them sight. The interesting thing about this story is that Jesus didn't just heal them, as He obviously could. He actually put the responsibility back on them with a single question: "Do you really *believe* I can do this?" (emphasis added) He was checking their faith. He knew that if they didn't believe, they couldn't receive.

I love how the next verse reads. Without hesitating whatsoever, the blind men said, "Why, yes, Master!" Then He touched their eyes and said, "Become what you believe."

When you get to a place in your life where you can boldly, confidently and without hesitation declare, "Lord, I believe in what I am saying about my life," then you will become what you believe.

If you're tired of the same circumstances year after year, but you believe in your heart that God has more for you, I know you'll be encouraged by Alanna's testimony:

> I have been inspired so much by Terri's teaching that last year I decided I could no longer live the same way I had for the past 34 years. In the summer of 2015, I took Terri's advice and decided to move out of Connecticut (where I grew up) and

move to Washington, D.C., and start a new life. I had a dream job in mind, and *I wrote down every detail* of what I desired and I got *really specific.* That was during the worst year of my life. I had to ignore current circumstances and go after what could be.

Each day, after spending time at work or with friends, I would determine to pack my room in boxes. I had lived with my parents all of my life (34 years) and I was tired of seeing other people with the ability to travel and afford their own place. I kept saying, "One day, one day. If only I had more money, that could be me." I had a defeatist attitude.

Then one day I realized, faith without works is DEAD. And I remembered, gee, I've never heard someone give a testimony where God blessed them tremendously and they weren't prepared. So I began to prepare. My family and friends probably thought I was crazy. I had been at my job

10 years and I was making less than my worth and I was tired of it. By the end of summer, I began to take trips to DC and apply for jobs. *Each day I incorporated action to my dream.* Summer came and went, fall came and went and I was growing weary, but I knew I couldn't stay in Connecticut any more.

I was about to give up but decided to apply for one more job. This job had everything I had asked God for! It is a dream job! I am learning how to professionally run a business from the ground up. My position was created just for me, a position that a recruiter told me couldn't and wouldn't exist. But God. Not only did God bless me with that job, God blessed me on my way out of Connecticut, like the Israelites leaving Egypt! My new place is brand new, every appliance, the floors, the bathroom, never been used! God put me in a wealthy neighborhood with all the amenities at an affordable rate.

My friends showered me with gift cards, my family blessed me financially, and a family member told me to purchase whatever I needed for my new place and she would pay for everything. I was thrown several farewell parties; it was like a wedding! *The very minute I set a goal and took action, God accelerated my blessing.* I'm crying while I write this because of how great God is. If we work the Word, it will work for us.

I reviewed my journal notes and saw that God had exceeded all that I had asked for. Job 22:28 says, *"You will also decree a thing,* and it will be established for you; And light will shine on your ways."

God had told me to *declare a new vision, a new life* for myself five years ago! And in the summer of 2015 I declared to everyone I knew, I was moving, getting a new job, a new life and so I did and here we are. *It wasn't until I believed* that God must bless me and that I must take action over my life that things began to change. So now I have time to plan more, dream bigger and never stop. Thank you Terri!

– Alanna M., Maryland

It is written: "I believed; therefore I have spoken."
Since we have that same spirit of faith,
we also believe and therefore speak.
– 2 Corinthians 4:13 NIV

Chapter Five
The 5 P's of a Personal Pep Talk

Success coaches worldwide teach the power of positive speaking or making positive affirmations. From hospital patients recovering quicker to plants being revived to life, words carry power! Research proves that positive words spoken over oneself can improve health, eliminate anxiety and stress, and bring an overall feeling of joy.

In fact, studies were conducted as far back as the 1920's when the jolly, French pharmacist, Émile Coué, treated hundreds of patients each day with a dose of *consistent affirmations*. Patients were simply advised to repeat the phrase, "Every day in every way, I am getting better and better," no less than twenty times each morning and twenty times each night. Astounded, thousands of patients reported illnesses miraculously cleared up on their own.

Simply put: your words create your reality.

It's not okay to be critical with yourself. Take an inventory of what you're allowing to roll off your tongue. Ask yourself, "Is what I'm about to say something I want to come about in my life?" If it does not line up with your dreams and desires, then don't voice it.

In the book of Luke, an angel appeared to Zechariah informing him that he and his wife were going to have a baby and instructed him to name the baby John. Overcome by doubt, Zechariah responded with unbelief, "Are you sure? Do you know how old I am?" Are you responding with the same negativity because of your current age? Are you questioning the dreams in your heart because you feel you're too old, too young or beyond the perfect time to seize opportunities?

Let's see how the angel responded to Zechariah's negative words. The angel said, "Because you doubted, you will remain silent and not speak until the baby is born."[18] He literally zipped Zechariah's lips! The angel knew that if he allowed Zechariah to speak his mind, he could forfeit the whole plan of God for his life. Think about that, for nine solid months Zechariah could not speak. That's how important our words are over our future.

Another powerful illustration is found in the book of Jeremiah. God gave Jeremiah a promise that he would become a prophet to the nations. Immediately, Jeremiah began to respond with words of inadequacy, "I'm too young! I can't speak to the nations!" God made no apologies in correcting his words, "Say not I'm too young!"[19] God knew that if Jeremiah spoke negative words he would seal his destiny. Consequently, Jeremiah changed the way he spoke, and it changed his future!

This book involves a two-step process: you've got to stop speaking negative, devastating, failure-driven words out of your mouth, but you've also got to proactively begin speaking positive, faith-filled, success-driven words as well!

Let's look at a few tips to help you get started making the right kind of declarations out of your mouth. I call them the 5 P's of a personal pep talk!

1. Positive

Avoiding negative statements is so important when you make declarations over yourself. Refrain from using words such as: no, not, never, don't, can't, lose, quit, stop, etc. Remember this key phrase: focus on what you do want, not on what you don't want.

Your words create mental images in your mind. When you focus on the negative, you are focusing on the very thing you don't want. For example, it's not as effective to declare, "I'm not overweight. I am losing weight." You are affirming what you're trying to get rid of. Declare the ideal weight you want to have not how many pounds you want to lose. "I am at my perfect weight of 125 pounds." That's a positive declaration of faith (if that's what you want).

It's important that you avoid mentioning the problem you desire changed. "I am getting out of debt," for example, still focuses on the negative impact of being in debt. It's more effective to focus on your ideal goal: "I am wealthy. I am prosperous. I am enjoying a debt-free life."

You might be thinking, "But I not telling the truth, Terri, when I make these statements. I'm not currently wealthy. I'm not at my ideal weight." I understand the concern about whether or not you're making up false statements that are contrary to your reality. This doesn't mean you walk around lying to all of your friends about your weight or your current income! But in fact, by speaking positive statements to *yourself* regardless of your current situation, what you are practicing is what God said in Romans 4:17. We serve a God "who gives life to the dead and speaks of nonexistent things...as if they already exist."[20]

You are simply practicing the character traits of God. You are exercising your faith by speaking of nonexistent things as if they do exist. Your words are more powerful than you may realize. Your words create your reality. If there's a dream in your heart, confidently speak it out in a positive statement.

2. Personal

You will identify with many scriptures and declarations in this book. I hope you will highlight them and begin to declare them over your life. You will notice that I have listed some of my favorite scripture verses in each section, but I have also made them personal.

When you personalize God's Word written straight to you, it's more intimate and aimed at your dreams. God loves nothing more than to hear His children take His Word personally and speak it back to Him.

Use the blank pages in the back of this book to compile your own list of declarations to speak over yourself consistently. It may include adopting a baby, learning a foreign language, acquiring a new skill, living in a certain city, etc. Make it personal to your life.

3. Present tense

Many times we are prone to making positive declarations about ourselves in the future. We make the mistake of thinking this is something that will happen much later. When we make statements like "I will make more money," or "I will get that new job," or "I will have a baby," it places your faith on the thought that one day, someday, just beyond reach, but not now!

We serve the Great I AM, not the great I WILL BE! I highly encourage you to begin your declarations with "I am..." (Or at least as often as grammar rules allow!) For example, "I am healthy. I am a best-selling author. I am beautiful inside and out. I am confident. I am full of courage. I am on time everywhere I go. I am an excellent leader."

You will notice a difference in talking to yourself *as if* you are describing who you are now...not who you hope to be one day.

4. Precise

You've heard the phrase "vague goals produce vague results." It's true with declarations as well when it comes to the *personal* dreams and goals that you have for your life. Yes, you need to make declarations like, "I am healthy. I am energetic. I am enthusiastic about my life." Additionally, the more accurate you are with your personal dreams and goals, the better the outcome. Doing this brings your mental picture into focus.

An example of a vague affirmation is: "I am making more money." Making more money could mean an extra $20. But if your goal is an increase of $10,000 in your salary, then say, "I am making an additional $10,000 this year." Specific declarations bring specific results.

5. Passion

The more emotion you have behind your declaration, the more effective it will be. If you simply go down a list of sentences reciting them in a robotic tone because some lady recommended you do this to succeed, you can forget it. There's no passion, no enthusiasm and no faith behind that. Read your declaration aloud with feeling! Simple recitation of words on a paper bears no consequence. It must have passion behind it. The more you commit to this discipline, the more your skepticism will fade and your faith will align with your words!

One of my favorite scriptures is Philippians 4:6, "Do not be over-anxious about anything, but by prayer and earnest pleading, together *with thanksgiving*, let your request be unreservedly made known in the presence of God" (WNT, emphasis added). How are you supposed to make your prayer requests and declarations of faith? With thanksgiving. Those two words mean more than we realize. When I declare my statements of faith, I thank the Lord with such enthusiasm that as far as I'm concerned, it's done! I express gratitude and appreciation for what God is *about to do* in my life.

I believe your passion, your strong belief in God's ability, touches the heart of God! When He sees that you wholeheartedly believe in what you're saying, remember, He sends angels to go to work on your behalf and make your declarations a reality! The angels are listening. They are on standby waiting to hear you speak faith-filled words so they can carry them out. Isn't that amazing? You don't want your angels to be bored all day, do you? Release your words of faith and expectancy with passion and watch what God will do in your life!

Practice the 5 P's of a Personal Pep Talk, and your life will follow your words!

Chapter Six
How Long is Long Enough?

Speak what you seek until you see what you've said. What does that mean? Keep doing it until it happens. It's that simple!

Chapter Seven
My Personal Daily Pep Talk

Earlier I mentioned how in 2007 I made a list of positive declarations to speak over myself every single morning. All it took was a little concentrated effort to think about what I wanted to declare and the consistency to do it. It's amazing how a 5-10 minute morning routine has brought drastic, undeniable change into my life. Below is a sample of my personal pep talk.

I am fulfilling 100% of God's calling on my life.

I confidently walk my calling out day by day.

I dream big dreams and believe that nothing is impossible to him who believes.

I set my hand to the plow, and I do not look back.

I am highly favored with God and man.

I am brought before great men because of the gifts God has given me.

I have fun doing what God has called me to do.

I am filled with and follow the peace of God.

I am in God's perfect timing in everything I do.

I am sensitive to God's voice, and I obey it quickly and quietly.

I am highly focused on my assignment, and I avoid all distractions.

I do not come into temptation, and I avoid the very appearance of evil.

I am disciplined spirit, soul and body.

I smile everywhere I go, and I look for opportunities to encourage others.

I love what God loves, and I hate what God hates.

I conform my will to God's will.

I am impacting this entire world for Jesus in a unique way.

I am a voice that inspires vision, confidence and discipline in lives around the world.

I am teaching people to fight fear with a plan.

I am a single-minded, focused believer, and I am stable in all my ways.

I am efficient with my time, and I stay focused on

my priorities.

I am unselfish and sociable.

I am extremely wealthy and constantly giving to others.

I lack for nothing.

I am creative.

I am confident, full of vision and disciplined in every area of my life.

I am an excellent model of godly leadership.

I have a spirit of discernment.

I do what I say I'm going to do.

I am surrounded by the best: big thinkers, big dreamers and big achievers.

I am always learning and growing.

I have the mind of Christ.

I am beautiful inside and out.

I am a woman of strong faith.

I operate in godly wisdom because I fear the Lord.

I attract God-inspired ideas that produce millions of dollars.

I receive God-inspired messages that impact millions of lives.

I am unique.

I am healthy.

I am fit, firm and muscular.

I receive invitations to minister from people I respect.

I am proactive.

I am committed to pursue and achieve my dreams and goals.

I am in the best physical shape of my life.

I am highly organized.

I am successful.

I am a bestselling author.

I am confident to speak on television.

I am confident to speak to live audiences.

I am an expert in the message God has given me to share.

I speak at the largest conferences in the world.

I am full of joy.

I am energetic.

I am convinced of my vision, my purpose and my mission, and I will not veer from it.

I am known for my giving.

I am merciful, and I receive mercy.

I walk in love and avoid strife at all costs.

I am a godly decision-maker.

I attract wealthy donors to the vision God has given me.

I am bold and courageous.

I have the gift of evangelism.

I am forgiven.

I am full of passion and enthusiasm.

I am anointed by God.

I am free in every way from anyone's and anything's control.

I am a voice impacting France for Jesus.

I am rescuing girls from human trafficking and providing the resources to renew their minds.

Keep in mind, most of these declarations were being spoken by faith because the reality was quite the opposite. Over time, I began to cooperate with my confessions and literally watched the changes take place. Is it a coincidence that what I am DECLARING I am EXPERIENCING? No!

There's Power in Praying God's Word

One of my favorite and most effective ways to pray is praying according to God's will. What is God's will? It's His Word. As I mentioned earlier, when you speak God's Word, you are praying His will right back to Him! Not only does it build up your faith, but His Word is living and active (Hebrews 4:12) and will not return empty but will accomplish what God purposed for it to do (Isaiah 55:11)!

As you consider making a list of your own declarations, think about those things that are most important to you. What is God speaking to your heart through His Word? As you read some of my own statements of faith, highlight the ones that stand out to you. This book is written to get you started. Look for declarations and scriptures that are most meaningful to you. Start with those and let it grow from there.

God reminds the prophet Jeremiah, "I am alert and active, watching over My word to perform it" (Jeremiah 1:12, AMPC). That's why the most powerful and effective communication with God is praying His Word! Prayers that bring results are prayers based on the Word of God. All we have to do is look at the story of Jesus in the wilderness being tempted by the devil to see how powerful the Word of God is. Every time Satan tried to get Jesus to sin or fall into temptation, Jesus used this life-changing tool to defeat the devil. He said, "The Scriptures also say," (in other words, "It is written") and He declared the Word. It sent the devil packing every time.

You might be thinking, "Where do I start? The Bible is such a big book. I feel overwhelmed!" That's exactly why I put this book together to give you a starting point. I used to hear messages like this and get stirred up inside because I knew it was the truth, but I didn't know which scriptures to confess or which faith-filled declarations to consistently speak. I would have good intentions to do the research of finding scriptures that applied to what I was going through, but never really got around to doing it. I'm going to help you out.

In the following chapters, my Pep Talks are split into sections that pertain to your future dreams and goals in the areas of finances, fitness, family, etc. The first one is a pep talk on your freedom. Personally, I couldn't even begin to go after my dreams for the future until I dealt with the past. I had to hear myself declare my worth, my value and my forgiveness before I could declare that I would impact a nation.

Based on your unique circumstances and aspirations, you may identify with certain sections more than others. Let God's Word speak to you as you read the scriptures, highlight them and start decreeing them.

I encourage you to keep your declarations and favorite scriptures before you. Tape them on your bathroom mirror, your refrigerator, your vision board, or on the dashboard of your car. Pretty soon, these words will get down in your spirit, and you'll know them by heart. When the devil attacks your mind, which he will (possibly before you even finish this book), the Word of God will come up out of you! And that is how you prophesy his defeat in your life!

Chapter Eight
Your Freedom Pep Talk

"The mouth of the upright will deliver them."
– Proverbs 12:6

You can't pursue your future if you're still hanging onto your past. The most important ingredient for success is having a healthy self-esteem. If you're like I was, consumed with insecurity, inferiorities and tremendous levels of fear and inadequacy, you can restore your damaged self-image with positive, faith-filled affirmations.

A positive self-image is seeing yourself the way God sees you and feeling good about yourself. If you are unable to respect yourself, you can't expect to courageously go after the dreams in your heart. Greater self-esteem leads to a greater life.

Don't Suffer in Silence
God wants to do big things in your life, but He can't if you

have a negative, insecure, inferior mindset. Any time God is ready to promote us to a new level, it always demands leaving a place of comfort and security. *You will have to leave your comfort zone* in order to achieve your dreams.

This reminds me of the story of four lepers sitting outside the city of Samaria (See 2 Kings 7). Thinking about their seemingly hopeless situation, they asked each other, "Why are we sitting here until we die?" It dawned on them that if they stayed where they were outside the city or if they went into the city where there was a famine, either way they surely would die. The place they were in represented transition. They were one action away from settling or thriving. Look up the story and you'll read how they got up and went after food and riches from the enemy's camp. God caused them to sound like a mighty army on the march against the enemy all because they got up and went after what belonged to them. They became fearless!

The moment you make up your mind that you're going after your dreams, you become a threat to the enemy! Naturally speaking, these four old lepers were not mighty men. They were tired, weak, hungry, handicapped men.

But they made a decision to stop living life defeated. They determined to go after the life God destined for them to have. That's what it takes to live your dreams!

Your freedom is found in your next decision. Are you going to sit by and watch others live their destiny while you waste away your potential? Or are you going to fight for what Jesus died to give you? Are you going to take the sword of the spirit, which is the Word of God coming out of your mouth, and fight back? Get up and fight!

What is God telling you to do? What has He put in your heart? Did God tell you to write a book five years ago? Did God tell you to apply for a scholarship? Did He tell you to believe for a promotion? Move to the mission field? Go on TV in your city? Are you supposed to purchase offices? Run for an election? Move locations? Resign a position? Build a house or a church? Launch a podcast? Start a blog? Open your own business? Launch a ministry? Support a ministry? Finance the gospel with your business? What you've done so far is NOTHING compared to what you're supposed to be doing!

However, your mind will try to talk you out of what God has put in your heart. You can literally think yourself right out of the will of God for your life. If you meditate on all your mistakes, you'll never fulfill your dreams. If you rehearse all your past sins, you'll feel incompetent to achieve your dreams. If you remind yourself of how unqualified you are, you'll stay where you are year after year full of nothing but regret.

That is Satan's plan. Remember, he is your enemy. He's not a Halloween character or a figure dressed in a red costume with a pitch fork. He's a real enemy who has one plan for your life: to kill, steal, and destroy you! (See John 10:10.)

What you've been through in your past is not coincidental. Your enemy hopes you'll remain inferior to others, intimidated by success and incapable of doing anything significant. Satan is a master deceiver, and he has a well thought-out plot to destroy every child of God. He would love nothing more than to stop your future. And he knows exactly how to do this—by keeping you trapped in your past, filled with insecurities and consumed with inadequacies.

"You were made for more!"
– Lisa Osteen Comes

God has placed in you everything you need to fulfill your divine destiny. As long as you're breathing, He is expecting you to have a vision for your life. God will come on the scene and help you fulfill your destiny, but you have to get a revelation of who you are in Christ. As long as you're carrying around negative baggage from the past, a poor self-image and low self-esteem, you will never live the life God designed for you to live. That's why you need to hear yourself declare your worth, value and who you are in Christ Jesus.

" . . . the lips of the wise will preserve them."
– Proverbs 14:3

Your mind will try to talk you out of what God has put in your heart. You can literally think yourself right out of the will of God for your life. If you meditate on all your mistakes, you'll never fulfill your dreams. If you rehearse all your past sins, you'll feel incompetent to achieve your dreams. If you remind yourself of how unqualified you are, you'll stay where you are year after year full of nothing but regret.

Quitting is Not in Your Blood

Years ago when I was going through one of the most difficult seasons of my life, I was feeling hopeless, emotionally wounded and on the verge of giving up. Giving up what? I don't know. I just wanted to quit. Typically, I keep everything inside and don't voice my struggles to anyone (except my best friend, Theresa), but this time, I was beat. I went over to my parent's house and admitted, "Dad, I just can't take it anymore. I feel like quitting."

I'll never forget my dad looking right into my eyes and saying, "The Savelles are not quitters. You're going to get through this. Quitting is not in your blood, you got it?" I just stared into space and said, "I think I'm adopted."

All joking aside, I needed that pep talk from my dad. His words brought hope, life, and victory on the inside of me. He gave me the motivation I needed to not allow Satan to gain any more ground in my thought life. I left inspired, encouraged and full of hope again.

I jumped in my car and drove home declaring who I was in Christ Jesus, reminding myself that God has already fought the battle for me, Jesus died on a Cross proving how valuable I am to Him. Not only am I a "Savelle" (and Savelles are not quitters), but I have the DNA of Jesus Christ!

In my book, *Make Your Dreams Bigger than Your Memories,* I detail how I obtained the freedom I enjoy today. Riddled with insecurity and feeling less than others due to some painful experiences, I had to begin making positive declarations based on God's Word or I would never be doing what I am today.

I began worshiping God for the very things I needed the most: peace, strength, comfort, wisdom, healing, and courage. I would magnify *Him* rather than magnify my messed up self-image. I worshiped Him for the very attributes that I needed the most in my life: Jehovah Rapha (our Healer), the Deliverer, the Prince of Peace, the Strong Tower, the Hiding Place, the Redeemer, and the Restorer of my soul. Nothing changed overnight. It wasn't an immediate transformation. But eventually, I was molded into a strong, capable, qualified (by God) leader and minister of the Gospel. My self-image began to line up with my declarations.

Since then, I have learned to keep myself encouraged every time the enemy tries to intimidate me with belittling or demeaning thoughts about my capabilities. And you need to do the same thing. You may have a tremendous amount of fear and insecurity that nobody knows about. You may be hiding behind a big smile like I was, but you don't feel worthy or good enough to do anything significant for God. You may feel like the least-likely candidate to pursue big dreams. Remember, God doesn't call the qualified, He qualifies the called. God is counting on you using the weapon He has given you (your mouth) to bring about change. God cannot use you publicly until you have gotten victory privately. But how do you get control over your thought life?

You Can't Defeat Thoughts with Thoughts

You defeat wrong thoughts with words, not with other thoughts. You can't try hard to think about something else until your bad thoughts go away. It's just a matter of time before your mind will go right back to where it wanted to be.

Imagine if I asked you to subtract 5,863 from 9,248. What if as you were subtracting in your head I interrupted you and asked you to give me directions to your house? You would have to stop working the math problem in your head to answer my question with your mouth. Your words, giving me directions, would take over the thoughts about the math problem. Try it.

Your mouth will cause you to go from constantly being under attack to being on the attack. When Satan comes at you with negative, oppressing thoughts, you will know how to shut him up. The answer is right under your nose. You just have to use it.

In order to gain tremendous freedom in your life, (freedom from the past, a poor self-image, low self-esteem, insecurities, fear, etc.), you must get comfortable making faith-filled declarations over yourself. You need to hear the Word of God spoken from your own lips. God's Word will heal your broken heart. He will improve your self-image. He will restore your joy. He will reignite your vision. He will refill your hope. There is no limit to what the Word of God can do in your life.

It's Time Fight Back

Do you recognize this famous movie pep talk?

> "And dying in your beds many years from now, would you be willing to trade all the days, from this day to that, for one chance, just one chance to come back here and tell our enemies that they may take our lives, but they'll never take our freedom!"
>
> – *Braveheart* starring Mel Gibson

It still makes me want to put on a kilt and grab a sword! Honestly, that's exactly how you fight back (minus the kilt). You need to grab your sword (which the Bible clearly explains in Ephesians 6:17 is the Word of God), and tell the enemy that he will never take your freedom! It's time to fight back by speaking faith-filled declarations over yourself and by giving voice to the powerful, limitless Word of God.

Freedom Declarations

I declare in the name of Jesus:

I am valuable to God.
I am chosen by God.
I am accepted and loved by God.
I am forgiven by God.
I am fearfully and wonderfully made.

I am unique.
I am confident.
I am bold.
I am fearless.
I am courageous.

I love and accept myself unconditionally.
I am beautiful inside and out.
I am healthy.
I am strong.
I am creative.
I respect myself, and I am respected by others.

I am favored of God.

I am wealthy.

I am always learning and growing.

I am sensitive to God's voice.

I have the mind of Christ.

I am funny.

I am fun to be around.

I am thoughtful.

I have the peace of God.

I am merciful.

I walk in love.

I am precious in God's eyes.

I am an excellent decision-maker.

I walk in humility.

I honor God with my thoughts, words and actions.

I enjoy studying God's Word.

I understand God's Word.

I have revelation knowledge of God's Word.

I love to worship God.

I love to pray.
I devote time with the Lord every day.
I am grateful.
I am humble.
I am loving.

I know God's voice, and I follow it.
I'm sensitive to the leading of the Holy Spirit.
I operate in the gifts of the spirit.
I walk in the fruit of the spirit.
I forgive those who have hurt me.

I believe in the dreams God has placed in my heart.
I am intelligent.
I am going to the next level.
I am being prepared for promotion.
I am qualified by God.

I have the courage to step out and pursue my dreams.
I am living life to the fullest.
I honor God in everything I do.
I am confident in who I am in Christ.

Personalized Freedom Scriptures

You are restoring health to me and healing me of my wounds, Lord (Jeremiah 30:17).

Thank You, Lord, that You go before me and You are with me; You will never leave me nor forsake me. I will not be afraid; I will not be discouraged (Job 7:19 HCSB).

The Lord is my refuge from oppression, my stronghold in times of trouble (Psalm 9:9 NIV).

I wait on the LORD: I am of good courage, and He will strengthen my heart (Psalm 27:14).

Lord, You heard my cry for mercy when I called to you for help (Psalm 31:22 NIV).

Thank You LORD, that You are close to the brokenhearted and save those who are crushed in spirit (Psalm 34:18 NIV).

I may have many troubles, but the Lord delivers me from them all (Psalm 34:19).

I cast my cares on the Lord and He will sustain me; He will never let the righteous be shaken (Psalm 55:22 NIV).

I find rest in God alone. My hope comes from Him (Psalm 62:5 NIV).

The LORD Himself goes before me and will be with me; He will never leave me nor forsake me. I will not be afraid; I will not be discouraged (Deuteronomy 31:8 NIV).

Thank You, Lord, for Your mercies and Your compassion never fail. They are new every morning (Lamentations 3:22-23).

I have sowed in tears but I am reaping songs of joy (Psalm 126:5 NIV).

I come near to God and He comes near to me. I wash my hands and purify my heart of all sin. I am no longer double-minded in Jesus' name (James 4:8 NIV).

Thank You, Lord, that You heal the brokenhearted and binds up our wounds (Psalm 147:3 NIV).

I choose to think on things that are true, noble, right, pure, lovely, and admirable—if anything is excellent or praiseworthy—I think about such things (Philippians 4:8 NIV).

The Lord surely took all my sicknesses and carried all my sorrows (Isaiah 53:4).

I humble myself before the Lord, and He lifts me up (James 4:10).

I declare that You are my God, so I will not fear. You strengthen me, you help me and you uphold me with your right hand (Isaiah 41:10).

I cast all my anxieties on the Lord because He cares for me (1 Peter 5:7 NIV).

I am confident of this, that He who began a good work in me will carry it on to completion until the day of Christ Jesus (Philippians 1:6 NIV).

God's grace is sufficient for me, His strength is made perfect in weakness (2 Corinthians 12:9).

Lord, I thank You that You hear me when I cry out to You and deliver me out of all my troubles (Psalm 34:17).

The weapons of my warfare are not carnal, but mighty through God to the pulling down of strong holds. I cast down imaginations, and every high thing that exalts itself against the knowledge of God, and I bring into captivity every thought to the obedience of Christ (2 Corinthians 10:4-5).

I thank You for consoling me and giving me beauty for ashes, the oil of joy for mourning, the garment of praise for the spirit of heaviness, so that I may be called a tree of righteousness, which You have planted, that You may be glorified (Isaiah 61:3).

Lord, I thank You that You are my refuge and strength—a very present help in trouble (Psalm 46:1).

I sought the Lord and He heard me and delivered me from all my fears (Psalm 34:4).

Greater is He who is in me, than he that is in the world (1 John 4:4).

I will not grow weary while doing good, for in due season I will reap if I will not lose heart (Galatians 6:9).

Chapter Nine
Your Faith Pep Talk

"Pleasant words are like a honeycomb,
sweetness to the soul and health to the bones."
– Proverbs 16:24

When I was a sophomore in high school, my parents enrolled me in a public school for the first time. After growing up in small, private schools, it was a big adjustment. After eight months of attending my new school, the Varsity cheerleader tryouts were announced, and I decided to go for it. As big, scary, and intimidating as it was, I had cheered every year in private schools, and it was my passion. I lived for Friday night football! The difference was I went from cheer tryouts at a private school in front of a hundred people to performing cheers all alone on a gymnasium floor (with my little voice) in front of *twelve hundred* high school students.

The night before tryouts, I remember walking outside

to my dad's garage where he loves to tinker with his classic cars. He knew I was trying out for cheerleader the next morning, and he could tell I was flat-out scared. I remember him saying, "Sis, you have the favor of God. Call on God's favor." He continued, "You can do anything you set your heart to do. Just go for it. Ask the Lord to favor you." I went back to my bedroom full of hope. I went to sleep, still a little jittery inside, but with peace that God was in control. He loves to favor His children especially when we call on Him. I remember lying in bed praying for favor. I believed it, and I experienced it by making cheerleader that year and the next. All because of a little pep talk and a little reminder of how good God is, from my dad.

"Transition is always God's way of promotion."
– Jerry Savelle

Many years later, after serving my dad for 22 years (11 years as his ghostwriter and 11 years as the senior vice president), I resigned my position as the CEO for Jerry Savelle Ministries International. It was the toughest act of obedience I've ever had to make in order to follow God's plan for my life. I knew it was right, but that didn't make it easy.

One day, after making the announcement that I would be leaving the organization and launching my own ministry 75 miles away, I was at home alone crying so hard. The idea of not serving my dad, not feeling involved in a ministry I had poured my life into, overwhelmed me with sorrow. Rather than keeping my feelings inside like I normally do, I texted my dad (because I couldn't speak through my uncontrollable tears) and said, "Daddy, I didn't know this would be so hard."

I'll never forget his response, "Transition is always God's way of promotion." Then, he added a faith-filled scripture from the Word of God that confirmed his uplifting text:

"And everyone who has left houses, brothers or sisters, father or mother, children, or fields, because of My name will receive 100 times more and will inherit eternal life" (Matthew 19:29, HCSB).

In other words, throughout the Bible, people always left GREAT things in order to have GREAT-ER things. "Transitions is always God's way of promotion." That's all I needed. I wiped the tears. Pulled my shoulders back. Held my head up and said, "Yeah, I'm being promoted!" That's a pep talk through a simple text reminding me of how good God is!

It would be nice if every time I needed encouragement, I could call my dad and say, "Okay, daddy, fire away! What does God's Word say? Build me up! Motivate me!" I mean, he is my dad. I can actually call him any time I want to, but how draining would that be? Pretty sure, as sweet as my dad is, he'd either teach me a life lesson on personal motivation, tell me to listen to one of his audio messages or change his number!

I've had to learn to become my own best cheerleader! I've had to realize that I can't wait around for other people to constantly be my inspiration. I've had to discover Who God is for myself and magnify His attributes in relation to whatever I'm facing. And you'll have to do the same. You have to learn to magnify God for Who you need Him to be.

The Nicknames of God

You may have nicknames that people call you. My family

calls me so many different names. Terra, Terra La Berra, Sissie, Susie Q, Red, and I'll just stop right there! And I answer to all of them. Well, throughout the Bible, we see God called by different names too. Some of His various names include:

Elohim – the Creator, mighty and strong (Genesis 17:7; Jeremiah 31:33)
El Shaddai – Almighty God or the God Who specializes in doing the impossible (Genesis 49:24; Psalm 132:2,5)
Adonai – Lord (Genesis 15:2; Judges 6:15)
Yahweh or Jehovah – ever present, near to those who call on Him (Psalm 145:18)
Jehovah-Jireh – the Lord will provide (Genesis 22:14)
Jehovah-Rapha – the Lord who heals (Exodus 15:26)
Jehovah-Nissi – the Lord our Banner as in victory (Exodus 17:5)
Jehovah-M'Kaddesh – the Lord who sanctifies or makes holy (Leviticus 20:8; Ezekiel 37:28)
Jehovah-Shalom – the Lord our Peace (Judges 6:24)
Jehovah-Tsidkenu – the Lord Our Righteousness (Jeremiah 33:16)

Jehovah-Rohi – the Lord our Shepherd (Psalm 23:1)
El Elyon – the Most High God (Deuteronomy 26:19)

This is not a comprehensive list of the names of God, but as you can see, He is many things. He is Whoever you need Him to be. He is your Healer, your Physician, your Miracle Worker, your Protector, your Counselor, your Strong Tower, your Hiding Place, and your Provision (to name a few). But you have to call on Him to be what you need Him to be. Calling on God gives Him the right to get involved in your circumstances.

Read this story of Mickey calling on the Great Physician to be her Healer:

In the fall of 2014, I was diagnosed with stage 4 breast cancer that metastasized to the ribs and spine. A very dear friend sent me Dodie Osteen's book titled, *Healed of Cancer*. I immediately read the book and knew I had to renew my mind with healing scriptures. Deuteronomy 30:19 says to choose life so that you may live. I chose life! God's Word is His will. There's a promise for every need in His Word. *I began speaking the Word over myself every day.* God's Word became first in my heart because it is life and health to the body.

I knew I could not let His Word depart from my eyes. My husband printed healing scriptures and placed them all over our home for me to see. My condition grew worse and death hovered over me. I continually confessed Psalm 118:17: "I shall not die, but live and declare the works of the Lord."

I knew God wouldn't lie to me and that He would keep His promises to me. Sarah judged God faithful for the child she bore. So I told God I too judged Him faithful to His promises of Divine health.

It's been nearly two years since that cancer diagnosis. I've been cancer free for a year. I'm not in remission which means temporary recovery, nor am I a survivor which means existing. The Word says I'm an overcomer in Jesus' name, healed by His stripes.

Nahum 1:9 says the affliction will not rise up a second time. I speak this verse every day along with about 60 other healing scriptures. The Word is constantly going forth out of my mouth to accomplish that which it is sent to do.

I memorized Psalm 91 and personalized it with my name and 'Papa God.' Some days I confess these verses several times a day. I'm alive and well! My Papa God is my Great Physician and His Word is my best medicine.

– Mickey B., Texas

Who do you need God to be in your life? Call on Him. That's how you demonstrate your faith in His ability to perform the impossible in your life. Declaring how big your God is builds your faith in His supernatural ability to perform miracles in your life!

Keep Your Eyes On God

I love the story of Jehoshaphat, a leader of the nation of Israel, told in 2 Chronicles 20. He was alerted by messengers that a massive army was on their way to destroy the nation. Jehoshaphat was stunned and didn't know what to do. He admitted to God that even if he did know what to do, he didn't have the strength to do it.

Still, Jehoshaphat sought God for direction, strength, and wisdom. When going to battle, he made an unexpected plan of action. He didn't send the best fighters to the front line. Instead, Jehoshaphat sent worshipers ahead of the army, almost like a modern day marching band. They magnified how big and powerful God was in the face of their biggest challenge. They didn't talk to God about their problem; they talked to the problem about their God.

"When he had consulted with the people, he appointed singers to sing to the Lord and praise Him in their holy (priestly) garments as they went out before the army, saying, Give thanks to the Lord, for His mercy and loving-kindness endure forever!" (2 Chronicles 20:21 AMPC).

In other words, when you feel you have no reason to magnify God, that's when you need to do it the most.

When you've lost a lot of money, your loan fell through, you didn't get the promotion and you've actually gained weight, that's when you need to lift your hands to heaven and begin praising God for Who He is and what He has promised to do in your life.

Look what God did when the people demonstrated their faith in Him through praise: "…the Lord set ambushments against the men of Ammon, Moab, and Mount Seir who had come against Judah, and they were (self-)slaughtered" (2 Chronicles 20:22 AMPC). This is such a bold reminder to us that the battle is the Lord's and the victory is ours. It doesn't matter how dim your circumstances look today, God is bigger. Let Him be your Counselor in the draining marital situation. Let Him be your Hiding Place when you need strength in solitude. Let Him be your Provider when it appears bankruptcy is inevitable or the bonus check is already consumed with unexpected expenses. God will be Who you need Him to be, but you have to activate your faith by calling on Him.

Remember, the Bible says, "For with the heart one believes unto righteousness (being right or whole), and with the mouth confession is made unto salvation"

(Romans 10:10 NIV, emphasis added). This shows us that it takes both the heart (believing, being fully convinced) and the mouth (speaking, declaring, decreeing) working together. The two combined, believing and speaking, will bring about the desired results.

It's not mind over matter; it's God's Word over the matter! God's Word always supersedes natural facts. Continually rehearsing how bad things are does not bring about positive change. Magnifying God will send confusion to the enemy and bring victory to your circumstances.

You Can't Defeat Goliath with Your Mouth Shut

"...I am God, and there is none like Me, declaring the end and the result from the beginning..." (Isaiah 46:9,10 AMPC). God wants you to do what He does. Declare the end result of what you are believing for before you ever see any sign of it happening. Your mouth contains power like no other weapon you have.

When you look at the story of David and Goliath found in 1 Samuel 17, the Bible tells us that Goliath *said* to David. You know, the devil speaks to us in the same way Goliath spoke to David. So what is our defense? Speaking back to him! Notice that David actually killed Goliath with his words before he ever released the stone:

"Then said David to the Philistine, You come to me with a sword, a spear, and a javelin, but I come to you in the name of the Lord of hosts, the God of the ranks of Israel, Whom you have defied. This day the Lord will deliver you into my hand, and I will smite you and cut off your head. And I will give the corpses of the army of the Philistines this day to the birds of the air and the wild beasts of the earth, that all the earth may know that there is a God in Israel" (1 Samuel 17:45-46 AMPC).

David spoke to his giant, the enemy, before he ever released the stone. He prophesied his enemy's death with the words of his mouth! You cannot defeat *your giant* with your mouth shut. Whatever giant it is in your life— your emotions, your weight, your money, your marriage, loneliness, anxiety, stress, depression, fear—whatever it is that tries to intimidate you, demonstrate your faith by speaking the Word of God!

Faith Declarations

I declare in the name of Jesus:

I am victorious in life.
I am more than a conqueror.
I am a world overcomer.
I overcome by the blood of the Lamb and the word of my testimony.
My faith is the victory that overcomes the world.

The favor of God surrounds me like a shield.
I have favor in the sight of all men.
God goes before me making the crooked places straight and opening doors that no man can shut.
I have the mind of the Holy Spirit which is life and peace.
I am spiritually minded.

I have the mind of Christ.
I am a believer and not a doubter.
I hold fast to my confession of faith.
The Holy Spirit leads me and guides me.

I am strong in the Lord and in the power of His might.

I have been created by God to prosper and make a difference in this world.
I am a success.
I am the head and not the tail.
I am above only and not beneath.
I am blessed coming in and blessed going out.

I am being transformed by the renewing of my mind.
I let the Word of God dwell in me richly.
I am meditating in the Word day and night, making my way prosperous and dealing wisely in all the affairs of my life.
The blessings of the Lord are overtaking me.
No weapon formed against me shall prosper.

I take my shield of faith, and I quench every fiery dart of the wicked one.
Greater is He Who is in me than he who is in the world.
I expect the best in life.
I am in the perfect will of God.
My faith overcomes anything that tries to overcome me!

Attributes of the Lord to declare:

You are my Restorer (Psalm 23:3).
You are the Lifter of my Head (Psalm 3:3).
You are my Hiding Place (Psalm 32:7).
You are my Wisdom (1 Corinthians 1:24).
You are my Shield (Psalm 33:20).

You are my Helper (John 14:16).
You are my Counselor (Psalm 16:7).
You are my Everlasting Father (Isaiah 9:6).
You are my Peace (Ephesians 2:14).
You are my Healer (Malachi 4:2).

You are my Hope (Psalm 71:5).
You are my Fortress (Psalm 18:2).
You are my Deliverer (Psalm 70:5).
You are my Strength (Isaiah 12:2).
You are my Rewarder (Hebrews 11:6).

Personalized Faith Scriptures

My faith is the victory that overcomes the world (1 John 5:4).

I will not throw away my confidence; for it will be richly rewarded (Hebrews 10:35 NIV).

My faith is sure of what I hope for and certain of what I do not see (Hebrews 11:1 GNT).

I believe that God will strengthen me with power through His Spirit in my inner being, so that Christ may dwell in my heart through faith (Ephesians 3:16-17 NIV).

It's impossible to please God without faith; therefore, I am a person of strong faith (Hebrews 11:6).

The God of hope fills me with all joy and peace as I trust in Him, so that I am overflowing with hope by the power of the Holy Spirit (Romans 15:13 NIV).

When I ask, I believe and do not doubt (James 1:6 NIV).

I live by faith, not by sight (2 Corinthians 5:7 NIV).

I know that the testing of my faith produces perseverance (James 1:3 NIV).

Whatever I ask for in prayer, I believe that I have received it, and it will be mine (Mark 11:24 NIV).

I pursue righteousness, godliness, faith, love, endurance and gentleness (1 Timothy 6:11).

I am watchful, standing firm in my faith (1 Corinthians 16:13).

I have chosen the way of faithfulness; I have set my heart on Your laws (Psalm 119:30 NIV).

It is written: "The righteous will live by faith." I am the righteous and I choose a lifestyle of faith (Romans 1:17 NIV).

Above all, I take the shield of faith, and I quench every fiery dart of the enemy against my life (Ephesians 6:16).

The Word says that if I believe, I will receive whatever I ask for in prayer (Matthew 21:22).

I fix my eyes on Jesus, the pioneer and perfecter of my faith (Hebrews 12:2 NIV).

I have been crucified with Christ and I no longer live, but Christ lives in me. The life I now live in the body, I live by faith in the Son of God, who loved me and gave Himself for me (Galatians 2:20).

My faith, without corresponding action, is dead; therefore, I take action towards my dreams (James 2:17 PHILLIPS).

I choose to fight the good fight of the faith (1 Timothy 6:12).

I am rejoicing that I have been justified through faith, and I have peace with God through my Lord Jesus Christ (Romans 5:1).

I remain on guard; standing firm in my faith; I am courageous and I am strong (1 Corinthians 16:13 NIV).

I walk by faith and not by sight; I practice faith (2 Corinthians 5:7).

My faith comes by hearing and hearing by the Word of God (Romans 10:17).

Jesus is the author and finisher (developer) of my faith (Hebrews 12:2).

Because of my faith in God, I do not fret or have anxiety about anything (Philippians 4:6).

I have faith that God is on my side (Romans 8:31 TLB).

My faith has made me whole spirit, soul and body (Matthew 9:22 AMP).

Declare Psalm 23 with Faith

The Lord is my shepherd, I lack nothing.
He makes me lie down in green pastures,
he leads me beside quiet waters,
he refreshes my soul.
He guides me along the right paths
for his name's sake.
Even though I walk
through the darkest valley,
I will fear no evil,
for you are with me;
your rod and your staff,
they comfort me. You prepare a table before me
in the presence of my enemies.
You anoint my head with oil;
my cup overflows.
Surely your goodness and love will follow me
all the days of my life,
and I will dwell in the house of the Lord forever.

Chapter Ten
Your Financial Pep Talk

**"This Book of the Law (the Word) shall not depart
from *your mouth*, but you shall meditate in it day and
night, that you may observe to do according to all
that is written in it. For then you will make your way
prosperous, and then you will have good *success*."**
– Joshua 1:8 (emphasis added)

It's God's will that you live a *prosperous* and *successful* life.
He wants your bills paid, your needs met and your bank
account blessed. You can enjoy a debt-free, financially
prosperous life, but you can also miss out simply because
you are not *speaking* in line with God's Word.

When we have serious financial challenges,
unexpected medical bills, unforeseen car repairs, broken
air conditioning units, school tuition notices, etc., our
natural tendency is to talk about the problem. It's human
nature to open our mouths with a big sigh and let out the

complaints: "Why does this always happen to us? So much for saving money this year! Of course, this breaks down! Right when I get my bonus check!"

As a Christian, you may *believe* that Philippians 4:19 is the truth, "My God shall supply all my need according to His riches in glory by Christ Jesus," but are you *speaking* in line with this truth? Or are you speaking what you fear, "I'll never get out of debt. I'm so tired of being broke. We never have any extra money."

Rather than secure poverty with your own words, God has given you the power to change your financial circumstances with your mouth. Instead of giving the enemy strength in your life by voicing how bad your credit score is, how high your debt is piling and how empty your wallet is, give God and the angels something to work with. Declare by faith, "I am debt-free in Jesus' name. I attract God-inspired ideas that produce great wealth. Opportunities and resources are headed my way now, in Jesus' name." Release the power of God into your pocket book.

That's exactly what Alisha and her husband did when facing what could have been a huge financial setback:

I would like to thank you so much for your ministry. My life and my family's lives have changed because of the encouraging message of your ministry.

At the time that I came to your Icing conference, so many of my dreams and visions had gone dormant. At Icing I was revived, awakened and encouraged. I listened to your messages over and over again. You asked us to submit our top 10 goals for the year to your website, and I did. I could literally feel the power of your prayers. As things were moving I just knew your ministry team was praying.

One of my visions (that I could not see *how* it would happen) was for my husband and I to be out of business debt this year and have money in savings by May 1st. We were in debt to the tune of $500,000 and it was overwhelming, but I knew God was able. We tried to get a line of credit against our house for part of the amount and could not get one, even though our house is paid for. I just wasn't feeling like more debt was the way we were going to be delivered from this. I struggled to come up with other business ideas and even considered finding a full-time job outside of our business or selling our house.

In one of your teachings you mentioned that we needed to *confess the Word of God and give the angels something to work with*. I finally decided to *stop complaining*, focus on where we were at and start declaring every bill is paid on time and that we are debt-free with money in savings. Your teaching really helped me to *change my words and expectations*.

How quickly the deliverance came! We had a piece of property that we thought was worth zero dollars—in fact we believed the property was a liability and we were going to have to spend money (that we didn't have) to restore it. Our partner in this property went to the register of deeds and assigned their interest in the property to us FOR FREE. They owned the majority interest in the property, 75%, and we owned 10%. I felt like they had stuck us with a liability, and I didn't want the property, but the Lord told me to stay quiet and not say anything.

A couple of weeks later, two large companies saw that we had received the property, and they both mailed us unsolicited offers for the property that were *enough to pay off all of our business debt and put money in savings!*

We received the final offer from the company to sell to on April 30th—just in time for the May 1st vision to be realized! It was finished! Yesterday, I picked up the check and closed on the transaction! Not only that, but this same company wants to buy another property from us that we thought was worth zero dollars!!

Praise God for His supernatural deliverance! He

is an awesome God. IMAGINE this—we did not seek the property and we did not seek the offer. I believe this is the first of many transactions like this. We have learned Kingdom principles. He truly does give seed to the sower. GOD IS AMAZING. Thank you for your discipleship. Our marriage has more unity than ever, our faith is built up, our prayer life has changed, we seek God for everything, our handling of finances has come into alignment with the Word of God. God bless you.

– Alisha K., Kansas

I'm not saying that you should just pretend that you don't have a stack of bills on your kitchen table. I'm not implying that your financial condition isn't real. I am saying that there's no power in rehearsing facts. There's power when you release your faith for God to go to work in your finances.

Attract God-Inspired Ideas that Produce Wealth

I shared a remarkable story in my book, *Imagine Big*, about when Rodney and I were getting ready to build our second home. At the same time, I was four months pregnant and eager to move into a bigger house. We had one snag. In order to reduce the monthly payment to an amount we could afford at that time, we would be required to put $48,000 down as our initial down payment! It still sends chills up my spine as I recall sitting in the builder's office, swallowing hard and assuring him, "Yes, we will have the $48,000 for the down payment by the deadline."

You have to know where we were financially at that time in order to comprehend what a gutsy declaration that was. We were living paycheck to paycheck and had $1,000 in our savings account! It was August of 1996, and we were scheduled to move in by January 30, 1997! How in the world could we come up with $48,000 in five months?

Rodney and I went home from that surreal moment and took a hard look at our finances. We recognized that all we had was $1,000 to put towards the down payment. Then my dad's words arose in my spirit and replayed in my head over and over: "You may not have what you need but you are never without the *seed* that will produce it."

"You may not have what you need but you are never without the seed that will produce it."

Rodney and I both agreed that what we had ($1,000) wasn't enough to meet our need ($48,000). So we changed our perspective from that amount being *all* we had to the best we had! Our $1,000 became our significant seed. We gave all of it away! We sowed the best seed we had. Now, $1,000 may not seem like much to you, but to us, it was very significant.

After we sowed that significant seed, we took a picture of the blueprints of our dream home and taped it to the refrigerator door in our kitchen. It became our vision board. Underneath the picture I wrote: "Thank you, Jesus, for $48,000 by January 30, 1997." Next, I listed the amount we needed in increments of one thousand:

$48,000	$38,000	$28,000	$18,000	$8,000
$47,000	$37,000	$27,000	$17,000	$7,000
$46,000	$36,000	$26,000	$16,000	$6,000
$45,000	$35,000	$25,000	$15,000	$5,000
$44,000	$34,000	$24,000	$14,000	$4,000
$43,000	$33,000	$23,000	$13,000	$3,000
$42,000	$32,000	$22,000	$12,000	$2,000
$41,000	$31,000	$21,000	$11,000	$1,000
$40,000	$30,000	$20,000	$10,000	
$39,000	$29,000	$19,000	$ 9,000	

PAID IN FULL!!!!!!

We kept that vision before our eyes daily. Then we declared, "Our God will supply all of our needs according to His riches in glory by Christ Jesus. Our needs are met. We're out of debt, and we have plenty more to put in savings. Our spirits attract God-inspired ideas to raise this money." We continuously spoke to this vision. Every time we opened the refrigerator door (and for Rodney, that's often!), we would speak it out loud.

I would drive home from work shouting and praising God as if the money was already in the bank. I was demonstrating my faith by thanking the Lord for the manifestation of our dream *on time*! We knew that we would have the money somehow someway. We had no idea HOW God would bring it about, we just knew He would.

Note: The number one question that will stop you from achieving your dreams is asking "HOW." Your job is not to figure out how your dreams will manifest. Your responsibility is to stay focused on the vision, speak to it, take action and trust God. Remember this: *When what you see inside becomes more real than what you see outside, it's just a matter of time. God will bring ideas, opportunities, resources and relationships to make your dream happen!*

And that's exactly what happened. God began bringing my husband and I both opportunities like never before to make money! We did everything from selling pinball machines found at a garage sale to ghostwriting books for other authors. Rodney went door-to-door painting address numbers on the curbs outside people's homes for money. I sold jewelry. I taught French to children after school. We seized every opportunity we could find to make money… and God continued to bring more opportunities.

Every time we were able to mark another $1,000 off the vision paper, we rejoiced! And yes, it looked quite scary when we still lacked $10,000 of our goal with only a few weeks to go! But God is faithful! As we proactively declared, "Thank You, Jesus, for providing all of our needs," the day came when we were scheduled to meet with the bank to prove that we had the amount needed for closing. We had earned $38,600 in five short months! However, the amount needed was $48,000. As we sat in the bank sweating a little bit, the loan officer came back to us and said, "After reviewing everything, it appears that your home has come under budget, and the down payment needed is $38,000 to move in!"

We had more than enough!

Whatever you are believing God for in your finances, declare it out of your mouth. Do it consistently. And take action!

> "The LORD be magnified,
> Who delights in the prosperity of His servant."
> – Psalm 35:27, NASB

Clarity is Key

I always encourage people to add intense clarity to their dreams and goals each year. Clarity is one of the single most important keys to success. In fact, as each new year rolls around, I challenge our partners and friends to get crystal clear on the goals they want to achieve by imagining it's December 31st of the new year. Looking back over the previous twelve months, what would need to happen in order for you to declare to your friends and family, "This has been the most amazing year of my life"? Whatever your response to that question is, those are your goals.

Be specific about your financial goals. As opposed to only writing, "I am debt-free in Jesus' name," I challenge you to calculate the exact amount. Write it down to the last penny. If you're believing for a car, be specific. Don't just expect any ol' car. Get a picture of the one you want and how much it costs. Once the vision is written down, you can either place it in your *Dreams and Goals Notebook* or hang it on your vision board. The point is to keep it in sight. You need to see it consistently.

Next, declare it out of your mouth. Thank the Lord ahead of time that your financial goals are met! That's exactly what Cathy did when she was believing for her husband's car:

> Just to share after listening to you, I have been clear with my prayers. So many of my requests have come to pass. Two days ago I specifically prayed for a newer car for my husband. His favourite colour is blue, and it had to be an automatic. He also asked for it to be a Mercedes!

> Yesterday, a member of the family rang (called) out of the blue and said that the Lord had told her to buy us a new car. It was for sale on her street, and it was a blue automatic Mercedes!! We picked it up today praise Jesus!
>
> – Cathy S., England

See It! Say It! Seize It!

These are not just things I teach, I practice them in my personal and professional life, too. For example, each Wednesday, I meet with my team at the office. The Bible says to "enter his gates with thanksgiving and his courts with praise,"[21] so we open every one of our team meetings with gratitude for all that God has done in our ministry. We go around the table with grateful hearts and voice what we're thankful for. Then we pray.

Next, we get out our "Top 10 Goals" for the year and we *declare them out loud* one by one around the table. Think about this, we are *seeing* them, and we are *saying* them fifty-two weeks a year! Is it a coincidence our goals continuously are achieved? My dad says, "See it. Say it. Seize it."

Carrie had a hard time understanding how God could increase her personal salary, but she continued putting her dream of a six figure salary before her eyes daily:

> I remember your story (among many others you
> have shared on podcasts) of Jim Carrey and Jack
> Canfield writing themselves checks for what they

wanted to earn. My goal was to earn six figures. This was one of my first goals that made it to my vision board. I prayed over it but got disappointed when it didn't happen right away.

It was hard to see how it could happen since I was making $85k at the time with no room for advancement in my current company. I gave myself time, but later changed the year in the memo from 2013 to 2014 and didn't even take the time to update to 2015.

I didn't fully give up though (thankfully, because I was so close). I took additional action toward my dream and met with a career coach and within 30 days (September 2015), I got a new job at a Fortune 100 company with an offer well beyond my asking salary!

I was apprehensive to ask for $103,000 but had a candid conversation with the HR manager about my rationale to which she explained that my 'salary requirement' *was lower than the job grade!* What?!?!

I knew then and there it was God. I continue to praise God for my salary of $110,000 with bonus potential of nearly $10k more annually. Only with God!

My life is on a completely different trajectory now! You are so right when you share how we must not give up and continue to fight and take action toward our dreams if we want to see them come to pass.

– Carrie N., Minnesota

Whatever you want to see happen in your finances, be specific. Call it forth! Speak it. Declare it consistently.

Finance Declarations

I declare in the name of Jesus:

I am blessed with an abundance of prosperity.
I am enjoying a debt-free life.
All of my needs are met.
I live to give.
I am blessed to be a blessing.

I receive the abundance God has for me.
I am a tither and a giver.
I am enriched in everything I do.
My personal income is increasing.
My savings account is increasing.

I am a wise steward with my finances.
I can be trusted with great wealth because I am a giver.
I am generous with the blessings God has given me.
I am an heir to the blessings of God.
I receive exceeding, abundantly, above all that I could ever ask or think.

I attract God-inspired ideas that produce millions of dollars.
I am a money-magnet.
Everything I set my hands to prospers and succeeds.
I honor God with my finances.
I have a growing financial portfolio.

I invest and manage my money wisely.
I am using the gifts God has given me, and they are prospering me.
I have more than enough.
God gives me ideas to produce great wealth.
I always have more than enough to meet my needs and to help others.

Unexpected money finds me.
I have checks in the mail.
God is my Source of supply.
I receive my divine inheritance from God.
My bank accounts are overflowing with financial increase.

I receive promotions, bonuses and raises.
I have an abundance mentality.

I have a prosperous mindset.
I have the generous nature of God.
Wealth follows me wherever I turn.

I owe no man nothing but to love him.
I am a wise planner with my finances.
I provide very well for my family and for future generations.
Wealth comes to me in miraculous ways.

Personalized Finance Scriptures

I seek the Lord, and I do not lack any good thing (Psalm 34:10).

My Father knows the things I have need of before I even ask Him (Matthew 6:8).

I honor the Lord with my wealth and from the first of all my increase; My barns are filled with plenty and my vats overflow with new wine (Proverbs 3:9-10 NASB).

I leave an inheritance for my children's children, and the wealth of the sinner is stored up for me (Proverbs 13:22).

I obey the words of God's covenant, so that I may prosper in everything I do. (Deuteronomy 29:9 NLT).

My God will supply all my needs according to the riches of His glory in Christ Jesus (Philippians 4:19).

When I give, it will return to me in full—pressed down,

shaken together to make room for more, running over and poured into my lap (Luke 6:38 NLT).

Thank You, Lord, that You delight in my prosperity (Psalm 35:27 NASB).

My God is able to do exceedingly abundantly above all that I ask or think, according to the power that works in us (Ephesians 3:20).

I don't worry about anything; instead, I pray about everything, telling God what I need and thanking Him for all He has done (Philippians 4:6 NLT).

He that supplies seed to the sower and bread for food, will supply and multiply the seed I have sown and increase the fruits of my righteousness (2 Corinthians 9:10 ASV).

The blessing of the Lord makes me rich, and He adds no sorrow with it (Proverbs 10:22 NASB).

The Lord shall increase me more and more, me and my

children (Psalm 115:14 KJV).

God gives me the ability to produce wealth (Deuteronomy 8:18 NIV).

I prosper in all respects, and I am in good health, just as my soul prospers (3 John 1:2 NASB).

I am blessed when I come in and blessed when I go out (Deuteronomy 28:6 NIV).

I will never be forsaken and will never beg for my bread (Psalm 37:25 NASB).

The Lord will give me prosperity. The Lord will send me rain at the proper time from his rich treasury in the heavens and will bless all the work I do. I will lend to many but never need to borrow. The Lord will make me the head and not the tail, and I will always be on top and never at the bottom (Deuteronomy 28:11-13 NLT).

I am a faithful person who will be richly blessed (Proverbs 28:20 NIV).

As I tithe, the Lord will open the windows of heaven for me and pour out a blessing so great I won't have enough room to take it in (Malachi 3:10-12 NLT).

You, Jesus, are the bread of life. When I come to You, I will never go hungry. When I believe in You, I will never be thirsty (John 6:35 NIV).

Chapter Eleven
Your Family Pep Talk

**"The soothing tongue is a tree of life,
but a perverse tongue crushes the spirit."**
– Proverbs 15:4, NIV

The greatest and most lasting gift you can give to your family is speaking God's Word in faith over them. You can personalize Scripture by inserting the names of your children or spouse and declare the Word of God over every aspect of their lives.

We know the Word was written by the Holy Spirit's inspiration and is full of power and hope. We also know God said His Word would not return empty (see Isaiah 55:11 NIV), so your prayers are based on a solid foundation. It doesn't matter what you are facing today in your family, with your spouse or with your children, God's Word is final authority.

If you have a spouse that isn't serving God, speak the Word of God over him/her. If you're believing for children, speak the Word of God over your body or over the right adoption. If you're believing for your family to come back to God, speak the Word of God. If you're believing for restoration, speak the Word of God. God's Word applies to every aspect of our marriage, children and families.

Read Courtney's story of how she used the power of speaking God's Word through her pregnancy:

> When my husband, Jason and I were believing for a healthy baby, I read through scriptures concerning that baby every morning and spoke them out loud over my body. This one was my favorite: Malachi 3:11, "and I will rebuke the devourer for your sakes, and he shall not destroy the fruits of your ground; *neither shall your vine cast her fruit before the time in the field*, saith the LORD of hosts." The part past the semicolon was the part that I had in bold and underlined. We would soon find out that it was twin boys that I was carrying! And they were healthy, carried to full term (not born before their time) with no bed rest!
> – Courtney M., Texas

I encourage you to bless your children every night before they go to sleep or every morning before they leave for school. Your faith-filled words carry power that can build them up and give them the confidence they need to walk out God's plan for their lives. Your words of faith cause them to walk in God's protection, provision and prosperity.

To this day, before I ever take off on a flight somewhere, I always text my parents to let them know where I'm headed. Without fail, they both text back, "We pray Psalm 91 over your flight." Psalm 91 is a powerful chapter on protection that I recommend praying over your household. I have provided it in its entirety at the end of this section as it appears in the Bible, but I have also made available a blank page for you to insert your family's name(s). You may want to tear that page out and place it somewhere in sight as a reminder of God's protection over your family.

Marriage Restoration

In previous books I've shared how my husband, Rodney, and I went through severe marriage difficulties and were separated for a season. We had so many unresolved issues from our past and getting married the way we did (being that I was pregnant before marriage). During our three-month separation, I was filled with mixed emotions—pain, anger, and definite unforgiveness towards myself and him. Everything had hurt me, including my own bad choices and bad attitude. I had allowed myself to become so calloused inside that I had no compassion for him. I flat-out didn't want to be married anymore.

Then I was reminded of the verse that says, "Forgive, and you will be forgiven" (Luke 6:37). I knew I needed to forgive Rodney if I wanted God to forgive me—and I needed God's forgiveness in a big way. It was a choice that absolutely had to be made. There was no room for excuses, but the truth was, I didn't want to forgive. One particular moment I vividly remember picking up a photo of Rodney and me on a vacation in Hawaii. I covered his face with my hand (not even wanting to look at him) and simply prayed in the spirit, walking circles around my den and kitchen. It was step one toward forgiveness. Believe me, praying in your heavenly language does wonders for bringing peace in a tumultuous situation.

Morning after morning, I repeated the process. I would

MAKE MYSELF pray over that photo. Gradually, my hand moved so that I could look at him and pray out loud. Finally, I could say, "In the name of Jesus, I choose—as an act of my faith—to forgive my husband. And I choose to forgive myself." That's all I was able to say, but I knew it had to be done whether we stayed together or not.

Stormie Omartian says that forgiving the person who hurt you does not make them right; it makes you free! I have firsthand experience that it is true. As I prayed over the photo of my husband and me every single day, I began to change little by little. Eventually, my anger turned to compassion. It didn't happen overnight. It didn't happen over the next week or even the next month. But it happened. I quit telling the story of my pain. I magnified God, my Healer, rather than magnifying my problems and complaints.

Faithfully, I read 1 Corinthians 13:4-8[22] out loud: "Love is patient, love is kind. It does not envy, it does not boast, it is not proud. It does not dishonor others, it is not self-seeking, it is not easily angered, it keeps no record of wrongs. Love does not delight in evil but rejoices with the truth. It always protects, always trusts, always hopes, always perseveres. Love never fails."

Eventually, I personalized it. Every place that I saw the word "love," I inserted my name to read: "Terri is patient. Terri is kind. Terri does not envy, or boast and is not proud…." Suddenly, I quit thinking about our past. I quit dwelling on it. I quit talking about it with others and began to dwell on God more than I dwelt on my problems until I was eventually healed…and so was my marriage. God has truly healed and restored our marriage. This year, as I write this book, we are celebrating our 25th wedding anniversary!

I am living proof that God's Word has the power to change even the hardest of hearts. But you have to speak it out by faith! The verses from 1 Corinthians 13 are at the end of this chapter along with a place for you to insert your name. I highly encourage you to take that step of faith and speak this powerful set of scriptures over yourself, regardless of your circumstances.

Be Specific About Your Future Spouse

These principles work in every area of life. You've read how they worked in my marriage, but let's read how Misty put into practice these principles of speaking over her future spouse and career:

Early 2011, I found myself at a dead end with my personal and professional life. I had been wasting two years of my life with a man I knew wasn't right for me. My mother kept telling me to make a list, write down the good and bad of the relationship. I put it off for months and months. The truth is, I already knew the good and bad, mostly bad, and didn't want to face the obvious truth.

Finally after going in circles with my life and relationship, I realized I had nothing to lose. My mom gave me a "Dreams & Goals" book that Terri wrote. She asked me to write down what I wanted in life, *pray over that list every day and speak it into existence.*

I made my list of what I wanted in my future husband. It was the opposite of the current relationship I was in. Within a couple weeks, I had ended that relationship and started praying over my future husband.

I had just recently started a new job and thought, *What a great time to also write down my vision for my career.* I have a high school education; I never went to college and for that reason a lot of people thought I couldn't amount to much. I was determined to prove those people wrong and challenge myself. I then made a list of my goals for work. I wanted to make six figures within a year, I wanted to be promoted and have favor with all my managers and be a top sales producer within the company.

Fast forward a couple of months...Every day on my one-hour drive (each way) to work *I was confessing and praying* for every single thing on my list, every detail of my future husband and the favor I would have within my job.

Within six weeks of working at my company, I

received a call from my manager that I was being promoted to the top sales department within my company. There were hundreds of sales reps at the company, and I was promoted to join only 30 of the top veteran sales reps. Within a year, I had not only hit the goals of making six figures but doubled it. I finished the following year being amongst the top 20 highest reps in sales for the company out of over 200 sales reps. Today, I'm still with the same company five and a half years later.

As for my future husband, I continued praying. In February 2011, I cut off all communication with my boyfriend and by June, I met my future husband. He was EVERYTHING I prayed for. I honestly didn't know someone like that was out in the world. I thought my list was a long shot but I thought I had nothing to lose.

We dated for one year and got engaged on our one-year anniversary and married 11 months later. He supports me in ways I didn't know possible; he always puts me and my needs before his own and loves me unconditionally. I never thought I would be able to be in a marriage like this.

The list and goals have only continued. We've written down new goals challenging us in our professional and personal lives. My husband listens to Terri's CDs and other great speakers on his 45-minute drive to work. It's inspired him to take risks and make career choices he would have never made had he not challenged himself. Listening to the speakers has changed his mindset to know anything is possible with God if you believe.

When I wrote my list in 2011, I started off with just a couple of things. Now after seeing God work in our lives, our visions are larger than life. We know now that with God, anything is possible. If God is for you, who can be against you.

– Misty E., Texas

You Have the Grace to Embrace Every Season

Regardless of where you are at this stage in life—single, married, divorced or widowed—as long as you're alive, God is expecting you to live a happy and fulfilled life achieving your destiny. You don't have to settle for loneliness because you lost a spouse. You don't have to be depressed because you're divorced. You don't have to be miserable because you have an empty nest.

In fact, I heard so many people complaining about their kids going off to college, leaving their house empty and depressing. Rather than accept (and even anticipate) sadness after Kassidi graduated high school, I began years prior to her graduation to declare, "I have the grace to embrace every season of life." When people would ask me, "Are you so sad about Kassidi moving off to college?" I would say, "She is my best friend, and I'm going to miss her. But I believe God's grace is on us both for this season."

My daughter is the dearest thing to my heart, and I am so grateful God has given us such a special relationship. Rather than fear sadness or declare misery, I intentionally declared the opposite. Children are designed to grow up and pursue their destinies as well. God would never intend for us to be depressed over the natural seasons of life. Consequently, the day Rodney and I moved Kassidi into her college dorm, I actually wore a shirt that said Grace across it and embraced God's grace in the moment. Yes, I cried when we drove away, but God surrounded me with peace, joy and the strength to send my daughter toward her destiny with ease.

Don't anticipate negative circumstances by speaking them out. Get on the offensive side and declare what you desire. Use this powerful gift God has given you to see victory, restoration and vision in your life.

Prayer for our families is the very foundation that keeps a family unit strong. You've probably heard the phrase, "A family that prays together stays together." Let me expound on that. A family that honors God's Word and His promises through believing them and speaking them will be able to withstand anything that comes against them.

Family Declarations

I declare in the name of Jesus:

The love of God rules and reigns in our home.
Peace is maintained and felt in our home.
The Holy Spirit is welcome in our home.
As for me and my house, we will serve the Lord.

My family is in the perfect will of God.
My family is healthy and enjoying divine health.
My family serves the Lord.
My family walks in peace with each other.
My family enjoys being together.
My family is honest with each other.

My marriage is becoming stronger, deeper, and more loving each day.
My husband/wife and I express mutual love, trust, and respect.
My husband/wife and I resolve conflicts quickly and respectfully.

My marriage is healed, healthy and made new.
My marriage honors God in everything we do.

I am a devoted spouse and parent.
I am forgiving and understanding.
I am patient and kind.
I am a great role model for my children.
I am easy to talk to.

I am consistently joyful.
I am grateful for each of my family members.
I am supportive of my family's dreams and goals.
I encourage my children/spouse.

We honor God in our home.
We walk in love and avoid strife at all costs.
We are loving and affectionate.
We are quick to forgive and let go of all hurts.
We enjoy laughing together and finding new ways to have fun.
We communicate openly and honestly with each other.
We love each other unconditionally.

Our home is full of joy and laughter.

Our home is experiencing restoration of everything that's been stolen.

Our home is a safe place.

Our home honors God in every decision we make.

Our home is blessed and favored of God.

I have the grace to embrace every season of life with my family.

Personalized Family Scriptures

I declare that as for me and my family, we will serve the Lord (Joshua 24:15 NLT).

Thank you, Lord, that You know the plans you have for my family—to prosper us and not to harm us, to give us hope and a future (Jeremiah 29:11 NIV).

Father, give each of our family members discerning hearts so that we may be able to distinguish between right and wrong (1 Kings 3:9 NIV).

My family looks to the Lord and His strength; we seek His face always (Psalm 105:4 NIV).

My family trusts in the Lord with all our hearts, and we lean not on our own understanding. In all our ways, we submit to Him, and He will make our paths straight (Proverbs 3:5-6 NIV).

We listen to advice and accept instruction, and in the

end we will be wise. Many are the plans in a man's heart, but it is the Lord's purpose that prevails over my family (Proverbs 19:20-21 NIV).

My family flees from sexual immorality. Lord, give us the understanding that our bodies are the temple of the Holy Spirit (1 Corinthians 6:18-19).

Lord, strengthen my family. Help us stand firm. Let nothing move us. I believe that we will always give ourselves fully to the work of the Lord knowing that our labor is not in vain (1 Corinthians 15:58).

If we lack wisdom in any area of our lives, we will always ask God, who gives generously to all without finding fault, and it will be given to us (James 1:5 NIV).

We submit ourselves to God. We resist the devil, and he will flee from us. We come near to God, and He will come near to us (James 4:7-8 NIV).

God is our refuge and strength, a very present help in

trouble for our family (Psalm 46:1).

In this house, we will not allow any unwholesome talk come out of our mouths, but only what is helpful for building others up according to their needs, that it may benefit those who listen (Ephesians 4:29 NIV).

Lord, may the words of our mouths and the meditations of our hearts be pleasing in Your sight, O Lord, my Rock and my Redeemer (Psalm 19:14 NIV).

I declare that my family is strong and courageous! We will not be afraid, and we will not be discouraged. We know that You are with us wherever we go (Joshua 1:9 NIV).

Father, You work all things together for the good of our family who love You, who have been called according to Your purpose (Romans 8:28).

Thank You, Lord, that You go before my family and You are with us; You will never leave us nor forsake us. We will not be afraid; we will not be discouraged (Deuteronomy 31:8 NIV).

I declare by faith that my family will not walk in the counsel of the wicked or stand in the way of sinners or sit in the seat of mockers. My family's delight is in the law of the Lord, and on His law, my family will meditate day and night. We are like a tree planted by streams of water, which yields its fruit in season and whose leaf never withers (Psalm 1:1-3).

Thank You, Lord, that You have given my family authority to trample on snakes and scorpions and to overcome all the power of the enemy; and nothing, shall by any means, hurt us (Luke 10:19).

We boldly declare that we will not fear, for You are with us; We will not be dismayed, for You are our God. You will strengthen us and help us; You will uphold us with your righteous right hand (Isaiah 41:10).

I believe that my family will not waver through unbelief regarding Your promises, but will be strengthened in our faith and give You glory, being fully convinced that You have the power to perform what You have promised (Romans 4:20-21).

I declare, Lord, that You are glorified in our marriage (Ephesians 5:25-29).

Lord, I pray that this family will never forget Your teachings, but we will keep Your commands in our hearts, and You will prolong our lives many years and bring us prosperity (Proverbs 3:1-2 NIV).

The commandments of the Lord are on our hearts. We instill them in our children. We talk about them when we sit at home and when we walk along the road, when we lie down and when we get up (Deuteronomy 6:6-7).

Thank You, Father, for restoring the years that have been stolen from this family (Joel 2:25).

Praying Psalm 91 Over Your Family[23]

He who dwells in the shelter of the Most High
Will abide in the shadow of the Almighty.
I will say to the LORD, "My refuge and my fortress,
My God, in whom I trust!"
For it is He who delivers you from the snare of the trapper
And from the deadly pestilence.
He will cover you with His pinions,
And under His wings you may seek refuge;
His faithfulness is a shield and bulwark.
You will not be afraid of the terror by night,
Or of the arrow that flies by day;
Of the pestilence that stalks in darkness,
Or of the destruction that lays waste at noon.
A thousand may fall at your side
And ten thousand at your right hand,
But it shall not approach you.
You will only look on with your eyes
And see the recompense of the wicked.
For you have made the LORD, my refuge,
Even the Most High, your dwelling place.

No evil will befall you,
Nor will any plague come near your tent.
For He will give His angels charge concerning you,
To guard you in all your ways.
They will bear you up in their hands,
That you do not strike your foot against a stone.
You will tread upon the lion and cobra,
The young lion and the serpent you will trample down.
"Because he has loved Me, therefore I will deliver him;
I will set him securely on high,
because he has known My name.
He will call upon Me, and I will answer him;
I will be with him in trouble;
I will rescue him and honor him.
"With a long life I will satisfy him
And let him see My salvation."

Psalm 91 Personalized

I encourage you to make Psalm 91 personal by changing the pronouns. We know that God watches over His Word to perform it. Praying Psalm 91 in a personal way makes it even more intimate and effective. It provides a powerful new point of view.

The more you pray it, the more it gets deposited into your spirit. Then when you need it the most, it will flow out of you.

Personal Psalm 91 Promise

_____ dwells in the shelter of the Most High, and he/she abides under the shadow of the Almighty. _____ says of the LORD, My refuge and my fortress: my God; in whom I trust!

For it is God who delivers_____ from the snare of the trapper and from the deadly pestilence (fatal, infectious disease). God will cover _____ with His pinions, and under His wings _____ may seek refuge;

God's faithfulness is a shield and buckler.

_____ will not be afraid of the terror by night or of the arrow that flies by day; of the pestilence that stalks in darkness; or of the destruction that lays waste at noon.

A thousand shall fall at _____'s side, and ten thousand at his/her right hand; but it shall not approach _____ .

_____ will only look on with his/her eyes and see the recompense of the wicked. For _____ has made the LORD his/her refuge, even the Most High, _____ 's dwelling place.

No evil will befall _____ , nor will any plague come near _____ 's dwelling. For He will give His angels charge concerning _____ to guard _____ in all his/her ways. They will bear _____ up in their hands, lest _____ strike his/her foot against a stone.

_____ will tread upon the lion and cobra; the young lion and the serpent he/she will trample down. "Because _____ has loved Me," God said, "therefore I will deliver him/her; I will set _____ securely on high, because _____ has known My name. _____ will call upon Me, and I will answer him/her.

I will be with _____ in trouble; I will rescue _____

and honor _____. With a long life I will satisfy _____
, and let him/her behold My salvation.

Declaring Love Over Yourself

1 Corinthians 13:4-8 (NIV)
Love is patient, love is kind.
It does not envy, it does not boast, it is not proud.
It does not dishonor others, it is not self-seeking,
it is not easily angered, it keeps no record of wrongs.
Love does not delight in evil but rejoices with the truth.
It always protects, always trusts, always hopes,
always perseveres.
Love never fails.

1 Corinthians 13:4-8 Personalized
Insert your name in place of the word "love" and "it."
Make this a part of your declarations and watch your
nature and personality begin to line up with your words.

_____ is patient, _____ is kind. _____does

not envy, _____ does not boast, _____ is not
proud. _____does not dishonor others, _____is
not self-seeking,
_____ is not easily angered, _____ keeps
no record of wrongs. _____does not delight in
evil but rejoices with the truth. _____ always
protects, always trusts, always hopes, always perseveres.
_____ never fails.

Chapter Twelve
Your Fitness Pep Talk

"The tongue of the wise promotes health."
– Proverbs 12:18

Does your mouth have anything to do with your body size? Of course. But most people focus more on what's going IN their mouths without any regard to what's coming OUT of their mouths when it pertains to weight loss and physical health.

I heard one medical doctor[24] say that telling yourself, "I'll never lose weight" has as much damage as eating a whole bag of chips. As you're reading this book, you might even be saying, "Positive declarations don't work for weight loss" which is a declaration in itself. Consequently, it *is* working in your life. What if you put as much focused attention on what's coming *out* of your mouth as what's going *in* your mouth in order to reach your fitness goals. I believe you'd reach your ideal physical weight much quicker. I know I did.

There's an old adage that states, "If you tell me the truth, I'll believe you. If you tell me a fact, I'll listen. If you tell me a story, I'll remember." I want you to read the stories throughout this book of people just like you and me who grabbed ahold of the Biblical truth that the power of life and death is in the tongue. Many of these people may or may not have even known the Biblical reference behind it, but they still saw results by changing their words. Read this amazing story of weight loss through a personal pep talk.

In his book, *What to Say When You Talk to Yourself*, author Shad Helmstetter tells of when he was overweight and struggling with weight loss for most of his life. He tried every possible diet and said all the wrong things to himself thinking his weight problem would never go away. He would diet, lose weight, gain it all back—plus more. Try another diet and repeat the process.

During his struggle, he began studying self-talk. He learned how some professional athletes competing in the Olympics had full-time self-talk trainers who literally gave them new messages about themselves and their potential to win!

Helmstetter thought to himself, "If Olympic athletes

can have full-time self-talk trainers to help them win gold medals, then what about the Olympics of weight loss?" With that, an idea emerged. He spent months writing his own affirmations and positive declarations over his weight loss and audio recorded himself reciting them.

"I decided to listen to them, playing self-talk in the background, while I was shaving each morning," said Helmstetter. "Every morning, I would shave, play the self-talk, shave, play the self-talk." Morning after morning, he repeated the process. "During the next ten and a half weeks, I lost 38 pounds shaving and playing self-talk in the background. And this time, I wasn't on a diet!" declares Helmstetter.

The equally remarkable fact is that during that same ten and half weeks of intentionally listening to his own personal pep talk each morning and losing weight in the process, Helmstetter's wife, who was putting on her make-up each morning at the same time, lost 25 pounds eavesdropping on his pep talk!

"That was over twenty years ago, and I've never been on a diet since," says Helmstetter, "I changed the program that caused the problem in the first place."[25]

Your words create your reality!

If you want to reach your fitness goals and enjoy your life, rather than be consumed with every calorie and tormented over food decisions, then become extremely disciplined in what you speak over your physical body. According to behavioral psychologists, as much as 77% of your self-talk is negative or working against you, and it takes as many as 20 positive statements about yourself to counteract one negative personal declaration.

The human brain can be compared to a computer. Once information is imprinted, the only way to change it is to erase it or replace it. Our minds work the same way with whatever information we have fed it or pre-programmed into it through our senses—our thoughts and the words we hear from ourselves and others.

Your subconscious mind believes what it hears most often. Studies show that self "trash-talk" leads to higher levels of stress and even depression. Most of us have failed time after time with developing good habits in our diet and exercise. When you, once again, make up your mind that you're going to eat healthier and exercise more, you still hold the guilt from your past of failing to keep your word or your commitment with yourself. Because of past experiences, you have a negative mindset from the start. This outlook reinforces the fact that you won't stick with it, you're prone to fail, and any little slip up is proof that you can't do it!

The instant you find yourself affirming negative statements and behaviors about yourself, STOP! Instead of using your words to *describe* how you feel, use your words to change how you feel. Let your words be what they were designed to be: a tool to help you reach your goals. James 3:4-5 tells us that a small rudder controls the entire direction of a ship the same way your tongue controls the direction of your life! Plain and simple, your words control your life, your outcome, your results, even your physical well-being.

Don't get me wrong, you may still think it, but don't speak it! You can curse yourself with your own words. It's not okay to be critical of yourself. Are you saying any of the following things?

- "I'm so out of shape."
- "I just have a slow metabolism."

- "No matter what I do, I can't lose weight."
- "It's impossible to be that size!"
- "I used to be in great shape."
- "Once you reach my age, it gets harder and harder to lose weight."
- "I hate my body!"
- "Obesity just runs in our family."

Well, stop! One of the ways we maintain our less-than-desired bodies is through the words of our mouths. Complaining and constantly focusing on the negative viewpoints we have of ourselves causes us to remain that way. Many overweight people jokingly say, "I'm fat. I'm lazy. I'm a couch potato," as a way of poking fun at themselves, but these statements are detrimental. It makes them part of your identity. Muzzle the inner critic once and for all!

The voice inside your head has a huge impact on who you are and what you do. If you were to give yourself a quick, daily pep talk, I am absolutely convinced it would uplift your spirit, increase your confidence, improve your overall well-being and eventually, impact your physical appearance.

In my book, *Dream it. Pin it. Live it. Make Vision Boards Work for You*, I told the story of my battle with maintaining my weight once I reached a certain age milestone. The voices around me were claiming:

- "It's harder to lose weight when you reach 40."
- "You won't be able to eat like you did when you were 30."
- "You have to work out twice as hard as you did when you were a teenager just to burn the same amount of calories."
- "You're about to reach the menopause stage, and you'll gain weight."

I had always been a fairly petite woman with a pretty good metabolism, but as I listened to those voices, I started to believe them. When I looked in the mirror, I started to dislike my thighs, my hips, my waist, my face… everything! My weight started to climb, and I became discouraged that I may never again "look like my old self."

For years I have exercised consistently, but all of a sudden no matter how hard I worked out or healthier I ate, it wasn't working! Maybe you can relate to the thoughts that were plaguing my mind, "No matter what I try, it doesn't help!" Those are debilitating thoughts. The more I believed it and expressed it, the more it became my reality.

Finally, I regained control of myself, my thoughts, my words and my attitude. I found a photo of myself at my ideal weight wearing a bikini, put it on my vision board (the one nobody saw but me) and looked at it every single day. In prayer, I would close my eyes and imagine myself looking like that again: my thin thighs, my trim waist, my flat stomach, my slender face, everything. Under the picture I wrote, "I am happy weighing 107-110 pounds."

My complaints were exchanged for positive declarations such as:

- I am grateful for my fast metabolism.
- I am in the best physical shape of my life.
- I am grateful that I can eat what I want and maintain my perfect weight.
- I am free from food and bondage to food.
- I am free from torment over my body.
- I am happy with my body.

- I am healthy and in excellent shape.
- I am thin, firm and muscular.
- I am disciplined.
- I am full of energy.
- I enjoy working out.

Then I began thanking the Lord for His promises to me in the Word of God.

Thank you, Lord, according to Your Word:

- The righteous cry out, and the Lord hears, and delivers them out of all their troubles. Thank You for delivering me from torment over my body (Psalm 34:17).
- In the multitude of my anxieties within me, Your comforts delight my soul. I am free from anxiety over my body (Psalm 94:19).
- Your grace is sufficient for me. I have the grace to weigh what I want to weigh (2 Corinthians 12:9). (Grace means the power of God coming on me to do with ease what I could never do on my own.)
- My body is the temple of the Holy Spirit. I choose to glorify You, Lord, in my body (1 Corinthians 3:16).

- I'm running hard for the finish line. I'm giving it everything I've got. No sloppy living for me! I'm staying alert and in top condition (1 Corinthians 9:27 MSG).

Astoundingly, the weight began falling off of me. The struggle was over. I began to transform into the very image of the declarations I was speaking and seeing on my vision board. Since then, I have thoroughly guarded my words over my body. I do not complain over my thighs. I do not express frustration over the amount of calories I consume. I do not deprive myself of something I want to eat. I expect to stay thin. I expect to maintain my ideal weight. I expect to have a high metabolism. And I constantly express gratitude to the Lord for giving me the desires of my heart.

If you are dissatisfied with your current health or overall body image, start by deciding what you want to look like. If you have a photo of you at your ideal weight, keep it before your eyes. Otherwise, find a pair of pants or a fancy dress in your ideal size and keep it in front of you as motivation to reach that goal.

Guard your mouth. Overeating is not nearly as detrimental to your weight goal as complaints are! Determine not to let one negative word come out of your mouth about your body again! I know it is not easy. We all have the tendency to look in the mirror and start to feel discouraged. Don't voice it. Your words are powerful and have a way of keeping you trapped in the very thing you don't want! Trade those complaints for praise and thanksgiving for where you are headed. Give God something to work with. All the weight-loss books and fitness equipment in the world won't change a thing until you first, guard your words.

My personal recommendation is to remove, hide or get rid of your scales. If you've gotten into a ritual of weighing yourself every morning and starting the day out discouraged and mad at yourself, stop feeding that disappointment with daily reminders. How would your daily outlook shift if you already weighed your perfect weight? How would your personal self-esteem elevate if you already reached your goal? How much time would you spend thinking about your life goals and dreams rather than wasting all that useless time thinking about food and calorie-counting?

Okay, if you absolutely cannot fathom life without that precious scale in sight, then at least write your ideal weight and tape it over the screen. Each morning when you balance yourself on that scale, enthusiastically declare, "I weigh my perfect weight!" And go about your day!

Whatever we say to ourselves will determine the state of our mind. What you dwell on, you become. Recently, I saw a video on the importance of positive self-talk by Greg Amundson involving an intense CrossFit competition of physical endurance. He told a remarkable story of the power of words when two athletes were finishing the final stage of a brutal fitness competition called a muscle-up station. In order to win the battle, they had to complete ten "muscle-ups." The two men, who were about the same height and weight, had been performing neck and neck all weekend long.

The final victory was up in the air as the competition was fierce. They were equally strong, capable and highly competitive athletes. Suddenly, something outrageous happened. As they approached the final workout of the competition, their mental state of mind and their choice of words would manifest results in an instant. You see, they each said something pivotal to their outcome. The first athlete ran by and enthusiastically said, "I've never done a muscle-up before. Today, I'm going to get my first one."

On the heels of the first athlete, the second competitor ran by and said, "I've never done a muscle-up before. There's no way I'll be able to complete this workout." Consequently, the two highly trained men went underneath the rings and got in position. According to Coach Greg Glassman, the founder of CrossFit who witnessed this competition, "They both secured a false grip (which was evident they both had the technical knowledge to perform the skill)." However, the athlete who said, only seconds before, "I will get my first one," pulled high on the rings, rotated through beautifully, and pressed to support himself. With a huge grin on his face, he continued to recycle ten muscle-ups in a row and await the competition.

The second athlete, with a defeated mindset and destructive self-talk who said, "There's no way I can complete this workout," never even got close to completing the exercise, and eventually gave up and quit. Glassman was amazed that with only three or four seconds passing before these athletes spoke their minds, one completed the skill; one did not.

Coach Greg Glassman said, "The greatest adaptation to Crossfit takes place between the ears."[26]

Your words matter. They affect the outcome you are experiencing. Your internal (and external) conversation with yourself either supports or undermines your progress toward your goals. You may not even be aware of the things you're saying to yourself because of how long you've been saying it. Too many times, we put more attention on what we don't want rather than what we do want.

Health surveys reported that individuals between the ages of 18 and 59 list a lack of time, a lack of energy and a lack of motivation as their top three reasons for being out of shape. They are very clear on why they haven't reached their goals. Typically, we back up our excuses with negative statements such as:

- "I might as well face it; I'll always be fat."
- "I can't get motivated to lose weight."
- "I don't have time to work out every day."

- "I don't want my mind consumed with counting every calorie."
- "I hate all these negative thoughts about my body."
- "I can't stand my thighs!"
- "I'm always so tired and exhausted."
- "I'm tired of not having any energy."
- "I don't like working out."
- "I hate feeling so out of shape."

These destructive statements become self-fulfilling prophecies. Basically, we talk ourselves into giving up. The point is that you are crystal clear on what you do not want. It's time to shift your focus on what you DO want. The Law of Attraction simply means that what you focus on, you attract. Proverbs 23:7 says, "As a man thinks in his heart, so is he." What you think about, you bring about. When you constantly declare, "I'm always so tired and exhausted. I have no energy," you are attracting more of the same.

After nearly two years of struggling with weight gain and a slower metabolism, discouragement and confusion over failed attempts to get a breakthrough in my health, once I began my own personal pep talk over my body, the struggle was over! That was years ago, and I have never struggled with my weight since! I am free from torment over food and over my body. I am free from struggling with weight loss. I am free to enjoy foods that I love (aka cupcakes). I am simply free. All along I thought the freedom was related to what I was putting in my mouth, but the breakthrough came as a result of what came out of my mouth! Plain and simple.

Change all the negative self-talk over your body to positive, capable, faith-filled declarations. Your pep talk creates your reality. It's time to rewire your brain and re-phrase your beliefs and declarations about your physical health. Let's start placing focused attention on what you DO want as opposed to what you don't want.

Fitness Declarations

I declare in the name of Jesus:

I am strong.
I am healthy.
I am in the best shape of my life.
I am beautiful inside and out.
I am free in my relationship with food.

I am fit, firm and muscular.
I feel good in my clothes.
I am happy with my body.
I have a fast metabolism.
I eat whatever I want to eat, and I maintain my perfect weight.

I am at my ideal weight.
I am full of energy.
I am dedicated to improving my health and fitness.
I am disciplined with exercise.
I look forward to working out.
I am easily shedding pounds and inches.

I am focused on achieving my fitness goals.

I see myself at my goal weight.

I have excellent stamina.

I am a picture of health and vitality.

I am enthusiastic about life.

I enjoy exercising.

I am free from food and from torment over food.

I am confident in my appearance.

I am enjoying a healthy lifestyle.

I am full of life.

I am lean.

I am radiant and youthful.

I am secure in who I am and how I look.

I am an excellent example of godly confidence.

Personalized Fitness Scriptures

So is my word that goes out from my mouth: It will not return to me empty, but it will accomplish what I desire and achieve the purpose for which I sent it (Isaiah 55:11 NIV).

God has not given me a spirit of fear and timidity, but of power, love and self-discipline (2 Timothy 1:7 NLT).

I can do all things through Christ who strengthens me (Philippians 4:13).

You satisfy me more than the richest feast (Psalm 63:5 NLT).

I prosper and live in good health even as my soul prospers (3 John 1:2).

I do everything for the glory of God, even my eating and drinking (1 Corinthians 10:31).

My body is the home of the Holy Spirit that God gave me, and He lives within me. It is a gift from God. He bought me with a great price, so I use my body to honor God (1 Corinthians 6:19-20 TLB).

I have already won the victory because the Spirit Who lives in me is greater than the spirit who lives in the world (1 John 4:4 NLT).

I am wise, and full of strength, I am a man of knowledge and grow stronger and stronger (Proverbs 24:5 NLT).

I am energetic and strong, a hard worker (Proverbs 31:17 NLT).

No discipline is enjoyable while it is happening—it's painful! But afterward there will be a peaceful harvest of right living for me when I train myself this way. So I take a new grip with my hands and strengthen my knees. I mark out a straight path for my feet so that I will not fall but become strong (Hebrews 12:11-13 NLT).

I will never forget Your commandments, for You have used them to restore my joy and my health (Psalm 119:93 NLT, TLB).

God is faithful. No temptation is irresistible. I can trust God to keep the temptation from becoming so strong that I can't stand up against it, for He has promised this and will do what He says. He will show me how to escape temptation's power so I can bear up patiently against it (1 Corinthians 10:13 NKJV, TLB).

I run straight to the goal with purpose in every step. I fight to win. I'm not just shadow-boxing or playing around. Like an athlete, I punish my body, treating it roughly, training it to do what it should, not what it wants to (1 Corinthians 9:26-27 TLB).

He gives power to the tired and worn out, and strength to the weak...Because I wait upon the Lord, He shall renew my strength. I will mount up with wings like eagles; I will run and not be weary; I will walk and not faint (Isaiah 40:29,31 TLB).

The God of peace makes me entirely pure and devoted to Him; my spirit and soul and body are kept strong and blameless until the day when our Lord Jesus Christ comes back again (1 Thessalonians 5:23 TLB).

Like an athlete, I exercise self-control in all things (1 Corinthians 9:25 NASB).

The thief's purpose is to steal and kill and destroy. God's purpose is to give me a rich and satisfying life (John 10:10 NLT).

I present my body as a living sacrifice, holy, acceptable to God, which is my reasonable service (Romans 12:1).

The fruit of the Holy Spirit is produced in my life: love, joy, peace, patience, kindness, goodness, faithfulness, gentleness, and self-control. I belong to Christ Jesus who nailed the passions and desires of my sinful nature to the cross and crucified them there. Since I live by the Spirit, I also follow the Spirit's leading in every part of my life (Galatians 5:22-25 NLT).

Everything is permissible for me, but not everything is beneficial for me. I will not be dominated or mastered by anything (1 Corinthians 6:12 BSB).

I have competed well; I have finished the race, I have kept the faith (2 Timothy 4:7 NET).

Chapter Thirteen
Your Future Dreams and Goals Pep Talk

> "The heart of the wise teaches his mouth,
> and adds learning to his lips."
> – Proverbs 16:23

In July 2014, five team members and I bravely drove out to Rockwall, Texas to search for potential office rentals as we were launching Terri Savelle Foy Ministries. Officially and reluctantly, resigning my position as CEO for my dad's organization, I was boldly obeying what God put in my heart and stepping out in faith to start my own ministry. As I mentioned earlier, I left a very secure position (and my comfort zone) in order to follow the dream in my heart.

As we drove around the beautiful lake town of Rockwall, Texas, we scoped out six or seven office spaces for rent.

One smelled of old people and borderline death. Another was, or had been, in the process of renovation with a toilet seat by the front door. And another was surrounded by a large field which meant it had field mice, and they were there to greet us as we casually walked in! Okay, I didn't make it past the front door as I screamed and ran back to the car (knowing full well that I could never work in an environment where rats felt welcome)! I'm cringing just remembering that one.

After hours of driving from one dilapidated location to another in search of something in our price range, we finally decided to take a lunch break at The Harbor Rockwall on Lake Ray Hubbard. Greeted by Mexican fiesta music, waterfalls and expensive yachts docked at the marina, we basked in the moment.

When we finished our Tex-Mex entrees and unlimited bowls of chips and salsa, we leisurely walked around the beautiful harbor buildings and boutique shops. Marty, the CFO of the organization, noticed a "For Rent" sign in the office space at The Harbor. Not even thinking we'd be able to rent it, we wanted to look at the space...and dream.

This was an eye-opener for me! As we toured the office

complex with our mouths wide open at the excellence of it all, not to mention the cascading waterfalls and scenic lake views, it dawned on me as the big-dreamer, faith-teacher that I am, "Why are we limiting God?" In other words, why are we acting like we can't even afford to ask how much this costs?! Why wouldn't God want the best for His children? Why can't we expect the favor of God to go before us? Why can't we have the best this city has to offer?

So, we asked. When we did, we discovered the office space for rent at this stunning location was the exact same price as the dilapidated building with the toilet at the front door! We could have settled for far less than God's best simply because we assumed we couldn't afford something that nice. But that's not all.

We signed a lease on the only section of office space they had remaining which was a very unique (aka strange) layout of offices. It didn't have a lobby, only a side door resembling that of a janitor's closet. A little sign we made read, "Terri Savelle Foy Ministries, please ring doorbell." It was a very creative use of space. But it worked, and we were grateful. However, I wasn't going to settle there.

I googled a photo of The Harbor showcasing the most beautiful office space available. It highlighted the Mediterranean style building and a rotunda with a 270-degree view of the lake and the cascading waterfalls surrounding it. I put it on my vision board and spoke to it every day. "I thank You, Lord, that we have the most beautiful space at The Harbor. We have favor with God and man. You are opening doors for us that no man can shut. Thank You, Jesus, for our offices!"

Each day, when I passed by that very space to get to my office, I would point to the elegant lobby with its marble floors and chandeliers declaring, "Thank You, Jesus, for our offices!" I didn't give God a deadline and was in no hurry. I wasn't expecting the current tenants to move out. In fact, they had signed a three-year lease only a few months prior. I wasn't trying to manipulate any pre-arranged agreement. I was simply practicing Romans 4:17 (calling things that be not as though they are) and trusting that God's timing is always right. Whether it's three years, five years or five months, I trust God.

Six months after we moved in at The Harbor, the office space next door came up for lease. It still wasn't the office on my vision board, but we took it. Six months after that, the nicest space available (with the beautiful lobby and rotunda) that I pointed to every day came up for lease. Unexpectedly, the tenants broke their multi-year lease and moved out. Simultaneously, God grew this ministry so much that we were ready to expand again. His timing was perfect, and we took possession of our dream office space!

I want to point out that this was not something I did once in a while or nonchalantly. I was confident God had reserved this space for our ministry, and I voiced it consistently. In fact, as you drive across the bridge into our city, you can see this beautiful office building on the horizon. Every time I crossed the lake, I pointed to the building and made my faith declaration. Once we signed the lease, my daughter said, "Mom, I've heard you say that so many times and now it's yours! It happened!"

What you are experiencing today is the result of what you have said in the past. And what you say today will be what you will experience in your future. Whatever you are believing God for, start speaking to it!

Speak to Your Dried-Up Dreams

In Ezekiel 37, there's a story of a man who faced a dead, barren situation, helpless to make any changes on his own. It was a literal valley of dead bones. God set Ezekiel down in the middle of them and asked him, "Can these bones live?" Picture this in your mind. There was no sign of life. It was all dead. He was looking at it and saw the proof. Nothing was happening. It was over.

Think about that in reference to your dreams. Sometimes there are so many negatives around us that it seems like everywhere we turn there is no hope to be found. The bank turned you down. No one is inviting you to come speak at their church or sing at their event. The publishers rejected your manuscript. The promotion was given to someone else. The ex-spouse has moved on to someone new. There are no visits to your website. Your own family thinks your dream is ridiculous, and now you're starting to think the same. It appears dead. It's over. God is asking you today what he asked Ezekiel, "Can these bones live?" In other words, "Can this barren, dried-up dream still live?"

In Ezekiel's situation, just like ours, that valley or

situation was over his head! He didn't have a clue how to make the bones live, but he knew who could. "So I answered, 'O Lord God, you know,'" (Verse 3).

In the very next verse, God gave Ezekiel the secret to resurrecting a dream: *speak life*. "He said to me, '*Prophesy* to these bones and say to them, "O dry bones, hear the Word of the Lord!""" (Verse 4). Notice the solution to giving life to death is in the words of our mouths. The next verse says, "So I prophesied as I was commanded; and as I prophesied, there was a noise, and suddenly a rattling; and the bones came together, bone to bone" (Verse 5). God gave them life again. And He will do the same to your dreams, but you have to speak to them. The dreams in your heart come to life by speaking words of life over them.

I've seen this in my life with obtaining buildings, securing publishers, speaking in specific cities in France, producing large sums of revenue, meeting and working with certain people I admire, and the list goes on. They didn't just happen; I had to speak them out! And you will too.

"Every time you speak it out,
you believe it in a stronger way."
– Joyce Meyer

"It's not enough to see it; you've got to speak it."
– T.D. Jakes

Future Dreams & Goals Declarations

I declare in the name of Jesus:

I am highly favored of God.

I am accomplishing everything God has placed in my heart to do.

I have the grace of God to help me accomplish my dreams.

I put actions behind my faith.

I am highly proactive.

I am courageous in the pursuit of my dreams.

I am sensitive to God's timing in my life.

I take bold steps of faith.

I am expecting breakthroughs in my life.

I am enjoying God's goodness and mercy.

I am overwhelmed by God's favor on my life.

I embrace every opportunity He brings me.

I am getting comfortable being uncomfortable.

I boldly step out of my comfort zone to obey God.

I have no fear.

I expect blessings to chase me down and overtake me.
I am surrounded by the big thinkers, big dreamers and
people of big faith.
I have more than enough.
I expect God to accelerate things in my life.
I am faithful to God, and He is faithful to me.

God is restoring the years that were stolen from me.
I am always in the right place at the right time.
I have extraordinary opportunities given to me.
I have preferential treatment because of God's favor.
I receive solutions to every problem, challenge and
obstacle.

I am God's most prized possession.
I am fulfilling my destiny.
I embrace every new season God has for me.
I am open to change.
I am talented and gifted with special qualities.

My gifts are going before me and bringing me before
great men.
I am thriving in life.
I choose faith over fear.
I have a sharp mind.
I have the mind of Christ.

I am equipped for everything God has for me.
I am rising above every obstacle.
I pray with boldness and confidence.
I trust God with my future.
I know that all things are working together for my good.

I am patient.
I am preparing for the next level.
I have a creative mind.
I am programmed for success.
I rise above every challenge stronger than I was before.

I have the wisdom of God to make the best decisions.
I let God fight my battles.
I live with purpose and passion.

I am a person of excellence and integrity.
I am fulfilling my life assignment down to the last detail.

Personalized Future Dreams & Goals Scriptures

I will be strong and not give up, for my work will be rewarded (2 Chronicles 15:7 NIV).

God is giving me the desires of my heart and making all my plans succeed (Psalm 20:4 NIV).

I delight myself in the Lord, and He will give me the desires of my heart (Psalm 37:4-5).

I trust in the Lord with all my heart and lean not on my own understanding; in all my ways, I acknowledge Him, and He shall direct my path (Proverbs 3:5-6).

I commit to the Lord whatever I do, and He will establish my plans (Proverbs 16:3 NIV).

I do not remember the former things, nor consider the things of old. Behold, God is doing a new thing in my life, and now it shall spring forth (Isaiah 43:18-19).

I can do all things through Him who gives me strength (Philippians 4:13 NIV).

I will not throw away my confidence; it will be richly rewarded (Hebrews 10:35).

I throw off everything that hinders and the sin that so easily entangles me. I run with perseverance the race marked out for me, fixing my eyes on Jesus (Hebrews 12:1).

God gives strength to the weary and increases power to the weak (Isaiah 40:29 NIV).

I am strong in the Lord and in His mighty power (Ephesians 6:10 NIV).

His grace is sufficient for me and His strength is made perfect in my weakness. (2 Corinthians 12:9).

God knows the plans He has for me, plans for welfare and

not evil, to give me a future and a hope (Jeremiah 29:11 NASB).

But one thing I do: Forgetting what is behind and straining toward what is ahead, I press toward the goal for the high calling in Christ Jesus (Philippians 3:13-14 NIV).

I remember the Lord my God, because He is the One Who gives me the ability to produce wealth, in order to confirm His covenant that He promised (Deuteronomy 8:18 NIV).

The Lord will accomplish what concerns me (Psalm 138:8 NASB).

This is the confidence that I have in Him, that if I ask anything according to His will, He hears me. And if I know that He hears me, whatever I ask, I know that I have the petitions that I have asked of Him (1 John 5:14-15). I will be exceedingly generous, and I will be exceedingly prosperous (Proverbs 11:25 NIV).

I will see the goodness of the Lord in the land of the living (Psalm 27:13).

Thank You, Father, for giving me spiritual wisdom and insight so that I might grow in my knowledge of You. I pray that my heart will be flooded with light so that I can understand the confident hope You have given me—Your rich and glorious inheritance (Ephesians 1:17-18 NLT).

I will not worry or have anxiety about anything, but in everything by prayer and petition with thanksgiving, I will make my requests known to God (Philippians 4:6 AMP).

Lord, You are my shepherd, and I shall not want or lack of any good thing in my life (Psalm 23:1).

The Lord delivers me from every evil work, and will preserve me unto His heavenly kingdom (2 Timothy 4:18). Thank You, Lord, that You are blessing me and enlarging my territory (1 Chronicles 4:10 NIV).

For God has not given me a spirit of fear and timidity, but of power, love, and self-discipline
(2 Timothy 1:7 NLT).

When I am weak [in human strength], then am I [truly] strong (able, powerful in divine strength). (2 Corinthians 12:10 AMPC).

I will not get tired of doing what is good. At just the right time I will reap a harvest of blessing if I don't give up (Galatians 6:9 NLT)

When I fall, I will arise (Micah 7:8).

And my God will supply all my needs according to His riches in glory in Christ Jesus
(Philippians 4:19 NASB).

Thank You, Lord, that You will bless the righteous; with favor You will surround me as with a shield (Psalm 5:12).

You prepare a table before me in the presence of my enemies; You anoint my head with oil; my cup runs over. Surely goodness and mercy shall follow me all the days of my life; and I will dwell in the house of the Lord forever (Psalm 23:5-6).

Your anger is but for a moment, but Your favor is for life; weeping may endure for a night, but joy comes in the morning (Psalm 30:5).

The Lord makes His face shine upon me, and is gracious to me; the Lord lifts up His countenance upon me, and gives me peace (Numbers 6:25-26).

Lord, You redeem my life from destruction, You crown me with lovingkindness and tender mercies, You satisfy my mouth with good things, so that my youth is renewed like the eagle's (Psalm 103:4-5).

God is able to make all grace abound toward me, that I always have all sufficiency in all things, and an abundance for every good work (2 Corinthians 9:8).

Blessed be the God and Father of My Lord Jesus Christ, who has blessed me with every spiritual blessing in the heavenly places in Christ (Ephesians 1:3).

I am so grateful that I can come boldly to the throne of

grace, that I may obtain mercy and find grace to help in time of need (Hebrews 4:16).

Everything I set my hands to prospers and succeeds (Deuteronomy 28:8).

Chapter Fourteen
Your Personal Pep Talk

**"Do not merely listen to the Word,
and so deceive yourselves. Do what it says."**
– James 1:22 NIV

I promise you, the more you do what the Word says, the more you will watch your life progress to the next level. Don't give up on God or His Word. It is the truth. It is the highest form of reality that exists. His Word never fails. If anything fails, it's our ability to stick with it. Just because your circumstances don't change overnight, don't give up. Get aggressive with your words.

Remember, every single time you declare faith-filled words out of your mouth, things are changing. Every time you get up in the middle of the night and praise God for Who He is in your life, things are changing. Every time you declare a scripture from the Word of God when you'd rather call up your friend to cry and complain, things are changing. Every time you look in the mirror and affirm what God's Word says about you rather than what your negative mind is thinking, things are changing. You may not see the changes yet, but you will.

As you begin to release your faith and speak in line with God's promises, expect the mountains in your life to be removed. Expect to walk in divine health, prosperity and protection. In the days and weeks to come, I am confident that you will experience more of God's favor, increase and success! Keep speaking and believing. Become your own best cheerleader!

Footnotes

1. Merriam-Webster 1828
2. TheRichest.com "10 Celebrities Who Shockingly Predicted their Own Death"
3. englishharmony.com
4. "Sorry to interrupt, dear, but women really do talk more than men (13,000 words a day to be precise)." http://www.dailymail.co.uk/sciencetech/article-2281891/Women-really-talk-men-13-000-words-day-precise.html
5. "Words and their stories: Where did 'OK' Come From?" http://learningenglish.voanews.com/a/ok--85357622/115551.html
6. "The Power of Words" https://www.youtube.com/watch?v=Hzgzim5m7oU
7. "How Olympians stay Motivated" http://www.theatlantic.com/health/archive/2014/02/how-olympians-stay-motivated/283643/

8. "The Champion's Creed" http://ruben-gonzalez.com/achievement/the-champions-creed/

9. "Top 7 Self-Empowerment Tips" http://top7business.com/?Top-7-Self-Empowerment-Tips&id=281

10. James 3:9-10

11. Genesis 1

12. Romans 4:17 AMPC

13. KJV

14. "A Controlled Trial of Arthroscopic Surgery for Osteoarthritis of the Knee" New England Journal of Medicine http://www.nejm.org/doi/full/10.1056/NEJMoa013259#t=article

15. Audioboom.com: Kenneth E. Hagin "God's Medicine 04 My Testimony of Healing"

16. NIV

17. See Matthew 9:27-29, The Message

18. Luke 1:11-20

19. Jeremiah 1:6-7

20. AMPC

21. Psalm 100:4

22. NIV

23. NASB

24. "Express Yourself: Your Mouth, Your Life" http://www.webmd.com/balance/express-yourself-13/negative-self-talk

25. "Self-talk and Why It Matters" podcast (23:00)

26. "CrossFit – Positive Self-Talk: The Greatest Adaptation" https://www.youtube.com/watch?v=wow114W-1jlQ

For years, Terri Savelle Foy's life was average. She had no dreams to pursue. Each passing day was just a repeat of the day before. Finally, with a marriage in trouble and her life falling apart, Terri made a change. She began to pursue God like never before, develop a new routine and discovered the power of having a dream and purpose.

As Terri started to recognize her own dreams and goals, she simply wrote them down and reviewed them consistently. This written vision became a road map to drive her life. As a result, those dreams are now a reality.

Terri has become the CEO of an international Christian ministry. She is an author, a conference speaker, and a success coach to hundreds of thousands of people all over the world. Her best-selling books Make Your Dreams Bigger than Your Memories and Imagine Big have helped people discover how to overcome the hurts of the past and see the possibilities of a limitless future. Her weekly podcast is a lifeline of hope and inspiration to people around the world.

Terri Savelle Foy is a cheerleader of dreams and is convinced that "if you can dream it, God can do it." She is known across the globe as a world-class motivator of hope and success through her transparent and humorous teaching style. Terri's unique ability to communicate success strategies in a simple and practical way has awakened the dreams of the young and old alike.

Terri shares from personal experience the biblical concepts of using the gift of the imagination to reach full potential in Jesus Christ. From stay-at-home moms to business executives, Terri consistently inspires others to go after their dreams. With step-by-step instruction and the inspiration to follow through, people are fueled with the passion to complete their life assignment down to the last detail (see John 17:4).

Terri and her husband, Rodney Foy, have been married since 1991, and are the parents of a beautiful redheaded daughter, Kassidi Cherie. They live near Dallas, Texas.

Terri Savelle Foy Ministries
Post Office Box 1959
Rockwall, TX 75087
www.terri.com

Other books by Terri Savelle Foy

Make Your Dreams Bigger Than Your Memories

Untangle

Imagine Big

You're Valuable To God

The Leader's Checklist

Dream It. Pin It. Live It.